MANAGEMENT

THE EXPANSION TRAP

HOW TO MAKE YOUR BUSINESS GROW SAFELY & PROFITABLY

Michael C. Thomsett

amacom
American Management Association

This publication is designed to provide accurate and authoritative information in regard to the subject matter covered. It is sold with the understanding that the publisher is not engaged in rendering legal, accounting, or other professional service. If legal advice or other expert assistance is required, the services of a competent professional person should be sought.

Library of Congress Cataloging-in-Publication Data

Thomsett, Michael C.
    The expansion trap:how to make your business
    grow safely and profitably / Michael C. Thomsett.
       p. cm.
    ISBN 0-8144-5954-4
    1. Industries, Size of.   2. Small business—Management.
I. Title.
HD69.S5T4   1990   90-128
658.4'063—dc20   CIP

Printing number

10 9 8 7 6 5 4 3 2 1

Contents

Preface   vii

Introduction   xi

I   The Big Picture

Chapter 1   Predicting the Problem   3
Chapter 2   The Expansion Ethic   27
Chapter 3   Focusing Your Objectives   44

II   Forms of Expansion

Chapter 4   The Volume Trap   67
Chapter 5   The People Trap   86
Chapter 6   The Geography Trap   106
Chapter 7   The Competition Trap   126

III   Solutions

Chapter 8   Valid Scorekeeping   141
Chapter 9   The Customer Service Approach   160
Chapter 10   The Expansion Kit   175

Index   189

Preface

Over the past twenty years, my attitude concerning business expansion has changed dramatically. When I first entered the work force as a junior accountant, I believed that *all* growth must be good. A few years—and a few jobs—later, I began questioning the value of expansion.

It was not the idea of a business becoming larger that concerned me, but the consequences of that expansion which many of my employers suffered. By the time I left the accounting profession in 1978, I had concluded that while expansion was a positive and necessary process, the methods of achieving growth were often flawed.

Since then I have worked as a self-employed accountant, an employee, a consultant, and now a writer. Looking back, I can observe common threads in the growth experience from the point of view of an employee as well as of a small-business owner. My interest in the topic of expansion comes from what I've observed and from how I've experienced the changes that come with business growth.

Not all the consequences of expansion are negative. In fact, the process should be a positive and rewarding one. The approach I take in this book is to discuss the aspects of expansion in as positive a light as possible. I believe that expansion is an exciting, challenging, and necessary process but that it has many ramifications. The most apparent form of growth is change in a company's financial status. We tend to define companies in terms of their sales and profits, number of employees, territories and stores, and competitive ranking. But of equal importance are the nonfinancial changes that occur as a business grows.

The book begins with an explanation of how to predict the problems that are confronted during periods of growth. Chapter 2 discusses the expansion ethic—a belief that growth is good and that the faster the pace of growth, the better. This is followed by an explanation of how to formulate and use a business objective.

Specific forms of expansion are explained in detail in Chapters 4 through 7—growth in terms of sales volume, personnel, geographic influence, and competitive posture. The last three chapters propose solutions to the expansion trap. Chapter 8 offers a system for monitoring and scorekeeping that includes both financial and nonfinancial tests. Chapter 9 proposes ideas for running a business with a customer-service emphasis. And Chapter 10 explains how business objectives provide the means for evaluating growth.

The topics are interrelated. Expansion is not a singular experience but, rather, happens on a broad front. As sales increase, changes occur in a company's competitive posture, internal staff, and financial reporting. Financial success, by itself, is only a small part of what really happens.

I also suggest identifying "growth plateaus" as important for planning and controlling expansion. When companies are aware of the changes that will come at the next plateau, they can be better prepared to get there successfully, and to expand beyond. The experiences of others who have climbed these growth plateaus are given throughout the book.

Through my observations, examples, and case histories, readers will be able to draw their own conclusions and set their own standards for expansion. These examples are compiled from direct experience and from the work situations in which I have found myself.

The significant point is this: I have seen many people succeed in their own business, and I have also seen people fail. In each case, the owners held common beliefs and brought common attitudes to the task of running a business.

But among the successful group, the owners understood that expansion had to take place on *their* terms. They had to be ready for expansion, and they had to be willing to prevent growth when the time wasn't right. And, of course, they knew their market and were willing to work long hours and dedicate themselves to making the business a success.

Those owners whose businesses failed seemed not to grasp a fundamental truth: EXPANSION IS NOT AUTOMATICALLY A HEALTHY OR A TIMELY PROCESS. This group suffered the consequences of the expansion ethic, which assumes that growth is always good and that today's problems can always be solved by expanding. The reality is that today's problems must be solved *before* moving on. We all appreciate the logic of this claim, but it's difficult to apply the idea every day—and it's too easy to lose sight of where one really wants to go.

In seeking solutions to the common problems faced in running a business and in planning and achieving an individual form of expansion, it is valuable to track changes beyond the financial. Are you in control of your own time? Are you putting energy into work you want to do? Are you satisfied with the experience of running your own business?

When you apply these less tangible standards, you increase your level of control over all aspects of the business. And that's what being independent is all about: being in control, creating the best environment for yourself, and expanding on *your* terms. In the final analysis, controlled expansion on a personal level is, perhaps, the most important form of growth.

Introduction

Sales are up. You're hiring people left and right. Customers are coming to you in droves. Now your biggest problem is keeping up with new orders. In fact, you're so busy you don't have time to do any planning. There's too much going on.

Nothing else can match the satisfaction and excitement of finding yourself in a rapidly growing business. Fears of failure, rejection, and having to return to employee status all evaporate and are replaced with confidence and the belief that nothing can stop you now.

Many small-business owners have reached this point, only to have it all come crashing down around them a few months later. Why does this happen? How can it be prevented? Those are the questions I'll address in this book.

As a business owner, you are under pressure always to beat a previous measurement of success. Like the sprinter trying to break the world record, you may fall into the trap of equating a new high point with success itself. While growth is necessary to every business, accepting growth just to exceed last year's record can lead to disaster. If the growth process takes over and runs the show, that's when the problems begin. Overhead creeps up and becomes permanently higher but sales levels vary. The nature of the business moves away from what you'd originally intended, making you a stranger in your own company. Or you're so busy dealing with one crisis after another that you no longer recognize the people on your payroll.

Some owners of growing businesses try to manage growth by spending more time tracking the numbers. You must assess and monitor financial information, of course; but you might do well to also concern yourself with broader objectives. How will today's decisions advance the business plan? In what direction are you moving? And what positive steps can you take today to make tomorrow's goals succeed? These questions can lead to far more valuable answers than those too-often-asked ones such as, What's wrong now? Whose fault is this? Why wasn't this done yesterday? This book shows you how to plan for growth and achieve it successfully, all on your own terms.

Let's start by defining some terms:

- *Growth* is a process involving change in several related ways. Future chapters deal with the specifics of growth attributes, including change in volume, people, geography, competition, and the internal structure of your company.
- *Small business* is an elusive term. I define *small* on the basis of annual sales levels and number of employees. Of 3.7 million corporate tax returns filed in 1987, eight in ten reported annual sales under $1 million.[1] And while a large proportion of businesses have few employees, I also define *small* as a business with fifty or fewer employees. Many of the examples in coming chapters deal with the challenges of growing in terms of employee base.

You may count yourself as a small business if your gross sales are less than $1 million and you have between zero and fifty employees. If you fit this description, you have undoubtedly considered what it would be like to operate on a larger scale.

To make objective decisions about when and how to expand, try breaking away from the common belief that you *must* grow or else your business is a failure. Question that assumption. Where does the pressure come from? And why must you seek growth now instead of later? In some cases, patience leads to greater expansion. In comparison, giving in to the pressure to expand can ruin a small business. An essential element of success is being able to maintain the independence and personal fulfillment that led you into your own business initially.

Here are some facts:

1. *Growth is not necessarily the same thing as success.* You may find that you're comfortable with a limited amount of growth, rather than with having to constantly expand sales, employees, territories, and competitive strength. A company that's profitable, manageable, and capable of delivering quality *is* successful.

The chapters dealing with volume, people, geography, and competition traps discuss how to pick the most comfortable size for your business today, and how then to go about achieving and controlling the timing and rate of future growth.

2. *Profits are essential.* You surely have heard of the "planned" loss, made acceptable because it represents an investment in greater future profits. As long as you're completely in control of growth, and have a precise plan for achieving it, planned loss is acceptable. But all too often losses occur because permanent overhead is created and not controlled. Profits *must* be earned if you expect to remain in business.

Two chapters explain aspects of financial results. Chapter 4 compares the relationship between sales growth and profits, notably how to create controls for overhead expenses. Chapter 8 shows how some of the common financial tests might not apply to your situation.

3. *You can remain small and still compete.* The idea that a small business will eventually be forced out of the market is not always true, as witnessed by the thousands of small-business owners who have identified a niche and who earn profits every year. Remaining small—or delaying growth until you're ready for it—does not necessarily mean dropping out of the success lane.

Chapter 3 helps you define exactly what type of company you want to create. Chapter 7 provides guidelines for finding your niche and dealing with the pricing, service, and other factors you face as a business grows.

4. *Success does not mean you have to get big enough to go public.* A popular misconception about success in business is that

you've only arrived when investors want to buy your stock. A small minority of companies ever expand to this point. Growth might be a positive and desirable accomplishment, but a small-business owner eventually has to decide exactly how big the company should become. You can succeed in business without aiming for a public offering.

The rewards of creating a business from nothing but an idea, and seeing it expand as the direct result of your efforts, are the most satisfying part of ownership. The pitfalls along the way can be identified, planned for, and avoided. This book shows you how to anticipate trends; what steps to take now to clear future hurdles; how to avoid growing too quickly or in the wrong direction; and how and why to work from a clearly defined objective and business plan.

Financial analysis is an essential practice for all business owners. You can't afford to overlook the numbers. But this book is about more than numbers. It's a guide for establishing a business plan to ensure personal satisfaction and success as well as financial control. Instead of preoccupying yourself with balance sheets and budgets viewed in isolation, here's a different course, a plan that you can live by and use to constantly evaluate growth opportunities. As a natural part of your personal growth, the plan will change with time and so will your objectives. By emphasizing personal satisfaction along with the bottom line, you can bring about future profits and quality expansion—in other words, success—as a logical result and outgrowth of your efforts. *Expansion* is not a bad word. But successful expansion is the result of advance planning, control, and faithful adherence to the rules you set for yourself.

Note

1. Internal Revenue Service, *Statistics of Income,* 1987.

I

THE
BIG
PICTURE

Chapter 1

Predicting the Problem

You have a tremendous advantage because your business is small. Unlike larger, more complex operations with many employees, territories, and overhead to control, you can directly nurture your company and quickly put your ideas into practice. As long as you stay small, a single decision can affect every aspect of your operation. And because you are in direct contact with your customers, employees, and vendors, *your own* personal efforts make all the difference.

As the size and scope of your operation grow, these advantages inevitably are lost. But that doesn't mean that you have to change your plan. For example, suppose you started your own business to provide exceptional quality and personalized service to every customer. That's still possible with growth, but maintaining that standard now demands more effort, delegation, and control. Your effective management style must be replaced with a less direct version of leadership. As your business grows, however, you will have to anticipate the expansion changes that can threaten your business.

Your flexibility and direct contact with all phases of your small business allow it to grow in good health. When every dollar counts, when every customer is highly valued and appreciated, and when the good work of employees makes all the difference between profit and loss, you can't help but play a significant role in shaping the business environment. And, of course, you fear losing that direct involvement as more and more responsibility is delegated.

Small businesses face a greater challenge in the future when attempting to expand, largely because it's becoming easier to gather information. With automated systems that are both affordable and widely used, you can expand your business at a greater rate than ever before. It's a lot like the changes the automobile brought about. In 1895, a salesperson could travel only as far and as fast as a horse could go. Fifty years later, sales territories were a great deal larger. So, too, only fifty years ago, information was compiled by hand; today, we use computers and fax machines. In the future, a business will be able to expand much more rapidly, if only because everyone is in closer contact with one another.

Ironically, technology has also made it easier to fail in business, because the speed of expansion can be greater than ever before. Failing in a business is not the final decree, however. In the United States a business failure is viewed more as a learning experience than a stigma. This is summarized by the Kiplinger Washington editors:

> Relatively few new firms become great successes, of course; the mortality rate has always been high in small-business start-ups, and this will be even more the case in a high-tech world. There is an enormous amount of churning going on in the newest sectors of small business, and for every success story there probably are a dozen-odd flops. But there also are a lot of comeback stories—the second and third tries that finally make it.
>
> To foreign observers, this is a striking feature of the American business scene—the fact that failure is a temporary condition, like a bruised knee, compared to the common situation abroad, where the social and financial liabilities associated with failure can be permanently crippling.[1]

Don't conclude from this that failure is acceptable, nor even that it must be expected. However, the risks to your reputation and public esteem are not devastating should your business fail. This point is important when planning for success:

> The common reasons for business failures are predictable, and the owner who is aware of the steps to take today will be able to avoid the pitfalls tomorrow.

Expansion in every aspect opens the door to possible future problems. But if you are aware of the ways that those problems arise and can recognize the signs of their approach, your business will survive, even in a rapidly changing environment. Any problem can be viewed as either a threat—in which case it's a definite negative—or an opportunity that, when recognized, can show you the way to a solution. How you address the problems as they arise will, in the long run, determine whether or not you will survive expansion.

Managing the Growth Plateaus

The life span of your business, like that of a person, can be defined in terms of growth plateaus. At each phase of its life, your business will experience a series of opportunities as well as a number of problems and risks to overcome. By identifying the growth plateaus, you will be prepared to deal with the problems that typify them.

Example: The owner of a rapidly growing jewelry business reached maximum capacity in her operation. It was time to expand inventory and seek professional assistance with the sales brochure. But the changes necessary to growth presented a new set of problems. The owner knew she did not have the management experience to ensure profits along with the greater stakes. She found help, though, through a friend who had operated his own business for many years and had gone through the same changes. She revised her business and marketing plan and budgeted her spending, established controls to keep expenses in line, and hired an accountant to help implement the changes.

Example: The owner of a small export company was losing interest in his business. He was working long hours, earning a decent profit, and finding a willing market demand. But the fun had gone out of the experience. What he finally realized was that he had become too comfortable. He was no longer excited about the future because, as he told himself, "There was no need to plan. Everything was working." He was no longer keenly interested because it had all become too easy. The required change was obvious: it was time to look for creative ways to grow—new markets and products, innovation in the method of reaching the customer, an improved edge on the competition. These were the exciting elements that had attracted him to the business in the first place. Now that he had an established base, the opportunity was better than ever. It only required his taking it.

Look for growth plateaus and anticipate the problems they present. For example, if you have set goals in the past and reached them, you know that the excitement is in the process and not in the result. Having achieved the goal, you need to go on to the next one. This is why expansion is the natural order of things—but also why the desire to continue expanding can cloud your vision, moving you in an ill-advised direction.

The solution? Look beyond your next plateau and make your plans accordingly. Be prepared to move from a realized *immediate* success to the next planned phase in your creative expansion. Remember that as the owner of a business, you have a great deal of freedom. Your creativity can be given free rein, and you can spend a great deal of time looking for the next opportunity.

Example: A consultant was deeply involved in gaining new accounts. His time was spend in meetings, in negotiating contracts, and in following leads. He was accomplishing his immediate goal, but he gave no thought to what would come *next*. Once he achieved his goal of getting new accounts, the consultant found it difficult to settle down and do the work. He fell into a depression. The solution came when he realized that the process itself was exciting, and he immediately set new goals. He dedicated one day per week to marketing, and divided his time between the exciting goal-building activity and the relatively mundane performance aspects of his business.

Example: The owner of a gift shop had plans to open a new store. At the point that the lease was signed and preparation was made for purchasing inventory, placing the first ads, and building the shelves and racks, she began planning her next move: expansion of merchandise into new lines. In this way, the successful opening would not leave a void in the owner's life. Another project would overlap, and its completion would become a priority.

Growth plateaus are not limited to achievement of specific plans. A small-business owner will also experience market capacity, changes in mental attitude, management problems, and a number of other potentially threatening plateaus—all of which can demoralize and rob you of a driving purpose or direction.

This is the classic problem that every creative business owner faces. The creative process is so exciting that having to settle down and simply manage becomes stifling. Just as employees can suffer from low morale, owners are susceptible to mood swings and disappointments. Once the goal is reached, once the problem is overcome, nothing worthwhile seems to remain. As psychologist and management consultant Judith M. Bardwick explains:

> People who have achieved something very difficult can become addicted to the struggle of accomplishment as well as the taste of triumph. The excitement is in the race to the goal, not in being there. Many of those people are no good at maintaining a system; they're only good at initiating and creating change. Their high is the creative start-up, beating the odds, going for it! Tuned to climbing the mountain to climb, they are existentially lost as long as they're still, even if they're sitting on the high plateau of success. They need a new mountain to climb, and life is flat until they find it.[2]

No matter what mountain you may have climbed, the only way to resolve this problem is to find a new, higher one. The trouble often is in following the need to achieve rather than sticking to the business plan. If you are addicted to success but ignore the pace of growth and the limitations in the market, you might be tempted to force an expansion that is neither timely nor appropriate for your operation. To balance these two concerns, the goals you set and the pace you follow must be controlled and planned.

Twenty Ways to Stay Healthy

Being aware of the need to keep yourself motivated will help you anticipate and overcome boredom. As a small-business owner, you need to remain motivated and interested. But this is only one of the challenges you will need to overcome as your business expands.

Every business owner can compile a list of problems that have been encountered. And in each case the list will be different. The suggestions given in Figure 1-1, and elaborated upon in the following sections, cover the most common areas for growth planning that require special diligence. Solutions to the problems raised are given later in this chapter.

1. *Remember the customer.* When your business first starts out, each customer or client is noticed and cared for. You know they must be nurtured and that loyalty results from living up to that customer's expectations. But as your business expands, the customer might fall to the bottom of the priority list.

If your time is increasingly devoted to putting out the fires that flare up in your operation, it's easy to view a new customer as yet another irritant—a factor that only adds to and complicates an already overloaded support system. Your perspective is then turned around. The customer's requirements *must* remain at the top of your priority list, no matter what internal problems you confront or how little time you have.

2. *Diversify your customer base.* If, by the nature of your business, you provide the majority of your product or service

Figure 1-1. Twenty ways to stay healthy.

1. Remember the customer.

2. Diversify your customer base.

3. Automate wisely.

4. Create profitable debt.

5. Stay humble and hungry.

6. Seek and take good advice.

7. Know when to get help.

8. Keep yourself fresh.

9. Remember your plan.

10. Guide yourself by the numbers.

11. Put controls into action.

12. Keep it simple and effective.

13. Change with the times.

14. Select risks – then take them.

15. Reduce risks with insurance.

16. Let staff know what's going on.

17. Use employee talent.

18. Use consultants selectively.

19. Watch your spending habits.

20. Plan tax liabilities.

only to a few customers, you face the risk of operating from too small a base. For instance, if your customer is a specific type of business, it's possible that most of your sales come from only a few customers—perhaps only one or two.

In this case, your entire operation is at risk of becoming a *de facto* employee entity. When only a few customers call the shots, you can't afford to jeopardize cash flow and profits by speaking out or by asserting your independence. Just as an employee can't afford to confront the boss in a way that might jeopardize job or career, the business owner cannot afford to alienate that one big customer. If you diversify your customer base, you provide your business with alternatives.

3. *Automate wisely.* If you begin with the assumption that your operation must be automated, you could be headed for expensive trouble. Automation is a tool primarily for processing information. The computer is able to handle volumes of similar information—to arrange it and organize your management tasks. But if you try to automate without justification or before volume demands it, you will end up spending many hours and dollars without profitable results.

Never begin by assuming a computer is essential to your operation. And don't try to automate because you aren't in control of a procedure. Those reasons for automation only result in bigger, more complex problems.

4. *Create profitable debt.* As your business expands, you eventually reach a plateau where further growth is not possible without outside financing. There is no fault in seeking loans as long as your debt is designed to produce profits.

Describing debt as "profitable" sets the criteria for borrowing. The test is logical and clear: you must be able to prove (both to yourself and to a loan officer) that the expansion plan will produce profits that exceed the cost of borrowing. Asking for a loan because you are experiencing cash-flow problems is not a solution; it makes the problem worse. And a lender will realize this, too; if you are having problems now, how will you free up the money to pay back the loan? You can't afford to expand until you first resolve cash-flow problems. Then you are ready to take advantage of opportunities for profitable expansion.

5. *Stay humble and hungry.* The two attributes that make the owner of a small business likely to succeed are humility and concern. Setting a modest objective for the first few months of an expansion project often is more important than dreaming of an international corporate empire. Remember the way it was when you first opened your doors? Every dollar in sales, every

customer, every hardworking employee, and every break was deeply appreciated. Strive to maintain the attitudes that enabled you to survive in the early phases of operations, and keep those attitudes alive, no matter how much your company grows.

6. *Seek and take good advice.* There is a great difference between pursuing your independence and failing to listen to sound advice from others. Many small-business owners have mistakenly come to believe that asking for help from someone more experienced betrays their claim of being able to "make it on their own."

Even when you have enjoyed many years of success, never become too successful to seek advice. Ask what others think, even when you don't believe you need the help. And if someone offers to help you, listen with all your attention. It doesn't hurt to hear what others have to say, even if it's criticism about the way you are running things. And if you're fortunate enough to find a mentor, listen especially closely to whatever he or she tells you. Experience, even someone else's, can save money, time, profits, and even the business itself.

7. *Know when to get help.* Don't allow yourself to get in over your head. The cost of learning management skills on the job is high—especially when your business is growing. When you need help, ask for it. Going to another business owner, a friend or relative, the U.S. Small Business Administration, or even an employee is no admission of failure. The only failure is in *not* seeking help when you really need it.

8. *Keep yourself fresh.* Small-business owners are creative people, if nothing else. That creativity is a refreshing, exciting, and rewarding attribute when applied to each situation you face. In fact, the freedom to be creative is probably one of the most satisfying experiences in running a business. You might discover, however, that in working longer hours under constant pressure, you forget to keep your sense of creativity alive. Don't allow conventional thinking to exclude your independence of mind.

There is a strong and direct relationship between an owner's creativity and his or her ability to build a workable objective within a plan. As business consultant Roger von Oech explains:

I've found that the hallmark of creative people is their mental flexibility. Like race-car drivers who shift in and out of different gears depending on where they are on the course, creative people are able to shift in and out of different types of thinking depending on the needs of the situation at hand. Sometimes they're open and probing, at others they're playful and off-the-wall. At still other times, they're critical and fault-finding. And finally, they're doggedly persistent in striving to reach their goals.[3]

9. *Remember your plan.* Guide every decision you make, every question and answer, and every direction you take so that it falls in line with your objectives and within the context of your business plan. Some owners put great time and effort into developing a plan, only to lose touch when the demands of daily operations increase.

Make time to plan. Everyone who has lived through a business failure will admit that the planning was incomplete or didn't exist at all.

10. *Guide yourself by the numbers.* The financial report is a summary of what's going on in your business. It's the score of the game. You must know the score, or you won't know whether you're winning or losing.

Whether you develop your own financial statements and analyses, or use the services of an accountant, set aside time to review the numbers. Find out what to look for and then follow up. Insist on timely reports that give you the information you need. Look for trends and be prepared to take action when a negative one appears.

11. *Put controls into action.* If you discover that cash flow is declining, overhead is rising, or that you are losing part of your market share, be prepared to take action. As long as you know your objectives and you have a plan, you will also know how to turn the trend around. This is essential. As an owner, your primary job is to control and anticipate.

Controls can be as mechanical as instituting cash or inventory counting systems, improving collection time, or using a purchase requisition. And they can be as high-level as identifying new markets, developing improved products or services, or putting together a customer-service program. Some controls can be delegated to employees; others will work only if you take action.

12. *Keep it simple and effective.* Entrepreneurs usually are unable to tolerate paperwork. They see the bigger picture, and would prefer to leave the accounting and analysis to someone else. But even the most entrepreneurial individuals, when forced into the management corner, are at risk. They may become bureaucrats in spite of their tendencies and motives. An attempt to improve the flow of information, for example, might lead to *more* paperwork; in fact, more paperwork means restricting the flow of useful information.

Entrepreneurs risk creating a bureaucracy or, equally as damaging, allowing one to grow around them. Even if the responsibility for tracking, analysis, and reporting is delegated to someone else, it's still necessary to keep an eye on developing systems and procedures. Keep it simple. Reduce paperwork. As your business grows, systems must develop and expand, but that can be achieved without sacrificing simplicity and effectiveness.

13. *Change with the times.* As a small-business owner, you might have found a successful, winning formula. You put it into practice and earned a profit. You repeated the formula, but then it stopped working. Instead, you need to keep an eye on change—in markets, in customers, and in demand trends. A winning idea this year might be obsolete next year. Change is constant, and you stand a better chance of survival when you're flexible and mobile enough to stay on top.

14. *Select risks—then take them.* Do you want to expand your product line? If so, when is the best time? Should you hire more employees, move to that bigger plant, lease that expensive machine? Owning a business means constantly making risky decisions. Actually, you face two problems: taking excessive risks or avoiding risks altogether.

It's a balancing act you must continually manage so that

you remain willing to take calculated risks appropriate to your circumstances while, at the same time, you recognize risks you can't afford to take. Expansion complicates this situation because bigger stakes mean greater risks. The danger is that you start to take risks you really don't want to take, failing to recognize the danger, or you become overly cautious and miss opportunities.

15. *Reduce risks with insurance.* You face an array of business risks by the very fact that your operation exists. Exposure to public liability, theft, natural disasters, fire, loss of health—all these could spell disaster. But the risks can be reduced or eliminated by purchasing the right amount and type of commercial and personal insurance.

When money is tight, one of the first expenses usually cut is insurance. But exposure to risk doesn't go away, and insurance is essential to the continuation of a business. You might not even be aware of some of the risks you face, so the services of an experienced, honest insurance broker will help you manage risk.

16. *Let staff know what's going on.* Your employees should be regarded as your most important resource. Yet if you don't communicate openly with them and don't include them in your plans, you could find yourself in competition with them. You have enough to worry about with other companies in the same business; don't alienate the people working for you.

Expansion invariably depends on the loyalty and participation of your staff. In many types of business you can't expand without people. So put an effort forth to develop, not only products and markets, but the all-important human resource as well.

17. *Use employee talent.* Nothing is as frustrating to an employee as being ignored. When talent goes to waste, discontent is not far behind. If this sounds familiar, think back to why you left your previous company. Don't make the same mistake with the talent right in front of you.

Employees are resources for growth, but that doesn't limit you only to developing their loyalty, paying higher salaries, or sharing your plans. *Really* including people also means identifying their abilities and putting those abilities to work. Give authority to those who deserve it, and let them run with it.

18. *Use consultants selectively.* Seeking advice from outsiders, even from a mentor, is a wise move for every business owner. But when you pay for that advice, be careful. Be wary of the expensive consultant who promises great results from streamlining, reorganizing, or "defining" your internal organization. These vague promises often cost a great deal of money and produce nothing.

Certainly, many management consultants can produce valuable results. But to protect your interests, enter into a written contract that limits the project and identifies the tangible results. Avoid the trap of hiring consultants as a cure-all for your operational problems.

19. *Watch your spending habits.* Expansion of volume can lead you to the common pitfall of spending carelessly. The more sales you generate, the greater the stakes—and the greater the need for close controls. Expansion means higher overhead and more risk of cash-flow difficulties.

Expansion should be accompanied with tighter controls, not looser ones. Never relax your watch over expense levels. Look for unfavorable spending trends and use expense budgeting wisely.

20. *Plan tax liabilities.* The successful, productive, profitable business pays a greater amount of tax than one with minimal returns. Thus tax planning plays an important part in the management of your operation.

With the traditional tax shelters virtually eliminated, how can you reduce your tax liability? By timing your purchase and sale of assets, selecting the best depreciation method, and deciding whether to report profits on a cash or an accrual method, you can anticipate and plan each year's tax liability. Also, tax avoidance is perfectly legal. You can take steps within the law to minimize taxes by deferring income, paying expenses a month early, or selecting the right accounting method. A capable accountant is a valuable ally in helping you save money with tax planning.

The act of expanding can, in itself, come to represent the greatest threat to the health of your business. In a society where growth is always perceived as good, we often forget that unplanned growth can—and often does—spell failure.

As a small-business owner who enjoys the freedom of achieving and who thrives on the creative process, you can solve this problem by identifying and pursuing *appropriate* challenges—new mountains to climb that do not threaten the methodical and planned growth of your business. Indeed, some owners make the transition from process to result with little trouble. Thus the entrepreneur becomes a successful manager and transfers the elation of climbing the mountain to the satisfaction of running the business well.

In many respects, the urge to set newer, higher goals can be satisfied through managing the day-to-day operation of a business—even without the risks associated with entrepreneurial activities. Suppose you attempt to run your own business. You may find your success is reward enough, and that your freedom is not inhibited by sitting behind a desk all day. Some owners, though, have little patience for what they view as mundane operations and prefer hitting the streets and beating the odds. For them, having to give up that excitement is too high a price to pay.

Example: When a bookkeeper quit her job and started her own service, she took a bold approach. Walking into each business establishment downtown, she asked for the owner, identified herself, and offered her services. This was frightening, and the rejections were discouraging at first. But as she began to meet with success, she started enjoying the initial contacts. She set quotas for herself, by the week and by the month. But the process became so enjoyable that, when it was time to sit down and do the books for her new clients, she did not enjoy it. She wanted to be back out there, selling her services to new accounts.

In this situation, someone who considered herself an administrative, not a sales, type discovered the fun of boldly approaching someone and selling an idea, something she preferred to the job for which she'd been trained. The motive for starting her own business was a desire for freedom, and not necessarily the desirability of keeping someone else's books.

As in the example, the entrepreneurial experience may uncover basic misconceptions or change perspectives. Upon realizing this, an owner with this type of problem has several choices:

1. *Recognize the transitional plateau and accept the fact that the primary service must be performed.* For example, the selling part, challenging and rewarding as it may be, is only one aspect of self-employment.

2. *Curtail the selling activity so that there is adequate time to complete the task.* For example, set aside one day a week to solicit new business. As part of this, set quotas so that the challenge remains, albeit on a reduced level.

3. *Enter into a revised plan calling for delegation of the routines.* In this way, the business can be built to a higher volume than originally planned. Management can be limited to supervision and review, while the owner spends more time selling and bringing in new business.

Each of these alternatives is acceptable, and each satisfies a requirement that you might have. For example, if you are willing to make a transition back to routine, the first choice makes sense. The second provides a degree of balance, and allows for moderate expansion that can be controlled over time. The third choice is the most aggressive, since it assumes you will be happy with a high-volume business and with little time in the office. This last choice demands better management controls so that accuracy and timely completion of tasks can be maintained at a high standard, but it also holds out the possibility of greater financial success.

Your choice must be made on the basis of the business objective you establish. If you want to grow slowly over time, and you develop management skills as a self-employed owner, you need to hold expansion at a level comfortable for you. If your objective is to aggressively pursue the market and grow as quickly as possible, be prepared to spend time reviewing trends, watching expense levels, and supervising the tasks you delegate.

Your Action Plan

Each of the potential problems you face in expanding—
whether derived from your own perceptions or from an operational change—must be anticipated and planned for with an
offsetting action. In anticipating expansion problems and arriving at a means for overcoming them, you exercise one of the
most important forms of planning.

The planning process is generally described in terms of
achievement, and it often refers to expansion itself. The expansion plan documents goals, such as higher sales and profits; a
larger plant; expanded markets, products, or services; or improved cash flow. But there is another side to the plan: the
anticipation and elimination of problems.

The following section lists steps you can take to anticipate
and counteract the problems commonly encountered with expansion. The topics correspond to the twenty methods for
staying healthy described earlier in this chapter, but they are
described as problems followed by solutions:

Problem 1: Forgetting the Customer

Description: Perhaps the greatest consequence of expansion is
the loss of direct contact with the customer. The number and location
of customers that your business serves have grown to the point that
personal care is no longer possible, and you expect this trend to
continue.

Solution 1: What is the customer's expectation of your product
or service? Will you be able to meet that expectation, even after your
operation grows? Anticipate the problems you will confront as your
business expands, and assign a responsible employee to ensure the
service your customers expect.

Solution 2: Survey your customers. Ask them whether they are
satisfied with your service and what improvements you should make.
Be accessible to your customers—in person, by phone, or by mail—
and ensure that all inquiries receive a satisfactory response. Never
promise action unless you know you can follow through.

Problem 2. Failing to Diversify the Market

Description: You originally intended to offer professional services to a variety of small and medium business concerns. However,

you now have two major accounts that together account for nearly 90 percent of your total income. This is of great concern, because losing either one would have a devastating effect on your profits.

Solution 1: Begin your efforts to locate new clients at once. There is strength and freedom in numbers. With only two major accounts, you can't afford to assert your freedom, because you can't afford to lose the business.

Solution 2: As you replace your dependence with reliance on more accounts, consider reducing the commitment to your two largest clients. Hire extra help and delegate those tasks, so that you will have more time for other clients.

Problem 3: Automating Too Soon

Description: You attended a computer show last week and saw a demonstration of a new menu-driven, user-friendly program for bookkeeping and several other applications. You want to buy the system, for which hardware and software cost approximately $9,000.

Solution 1: Take a professional approach to looking at computers. First identify the operations that can be more efficiently done on a computer. If the volume in your bookkeeping is fairly low, you do *not* need to automate it; that's a large investment for no value. Your staff will have to learn how to operate the system, so it won't save any time. If you want to automate because you're having problems, you are only asking for more trouble; first solve the problem, then consider whether a computer will save you money.

Solution 2: Forget the notion that a computer is mandatory for you to remain in business. That's only true when the cost of processing a large number of similar transactions is higher than what your competitors must pay and, thus, they can price the goods or services lower than you can.

Problem 4: Assuming Too Much Debt

Description: You have reached a growth plateau after four years in business. To expand beyond this point, you need larger facilities, more staff, and better equipment. Even though you've grown substantially, you still have a problem with cash flow. A loan might help.

Solution 1: If you're having cash-flow problems without carrying any debt, those problems will only multiply when you're committed to monthly payments. Ask your accountant for help in getting the cash flow into a healthier state—*before* applying for a loan.

Solution 2: Study the profitability of borrowing money as part of a revised business plan. Ask yourself: Will a loan enable me to produce future profits greater than the interest cost of borrowing? Before asking for a loan, prove that the opportunity exists to earn a net after-interest profit.

Problem 5: Relaxing Your Diligence

Description: When you started your business, you had modest goals, which you have now surpassed. You sense that you're not as hungry for business as you once were, and that you might be becoming too relaxed.

Solution 1: Set aside time to reevaluate your objective and review the direction you're taking.

Solution 2: List your future objectives and develop a plan for implementing them.

Problem 6: Failing to Take Good Advice

Description: You are strong-willed and opinionated. At times, you find yourself thinking you have it all figured out, and you resist when others try to advise you.

Solution 1: Acknowledge the reality that no one has all the answers, and you need advice and other points of view.

Solution 2: Make a point of asking for advice from others, even when you *think* you already know the answer.

Problem 7: Refusing to Get Help

Description: Getting in over your head is extremely easy to do, but pulling yourself out is much more difficult. This is a failure to recognize your own management limits, or to accept the reality that no one person can address every issue alone.

Solution 1: List your strong and weak points. Which weak points will demand management talent in the near future? Determine whether you will need to hire help or should acquire the skills you will need.

Solution 2: Take action before the problem gets out of hand. For example, suppose you have decided to hire a number of employees, but you do not enjoy supervision. Hire an office manager before the problem becomes worse.

Problem 8: Loss of Creativity

Description: The demands of day-to-day work have distracted you from your original reasons for starting the business, which were to set your own course and achieve your objectives in creative ways. You find yourself becoming a conservative manager.

Solution 1: Seek creative outlets, even if you are limited to running the business and do not have a great deal of time to plan.

Solution 2: Set aside a specific time each week, away from phones, appointments, and meetings, to quietly plan. Use your creativity to examine and anticipate the direction of your operation.

Problem 9: Forgetting the Plan

Description: You developed a business plan and a clear objective, but now the plan is not being used. Either you have achieved your original modest goals and have not updated the plan, or you were distracted with more immediate concerns.

Solution 1: Write a new business plan. This should be a high priority, because you never outgrow the need to plan or to revise yesterday's ideas. As expansion begins to occur, your business plan must be a blueprint for achieving your objectives.

Solution 2: Put a review procedure into effect. Look at your plan at least once a week and compare your deadlines to the progress actually being made. Watch trends and anticipate problems, and then take needed actions to keep on track.

Problem 10: Ignoring the Numbers

Description: Your business succeeded for the first year or two without financial review, budgets, or trend analyses. You expect exceptional growth in the coming year, which means higher costs and the need for greater planning of expenses and cash flow.

Solution 1: Prepare an income forecast and expense budget; also map out your expectations of cash flow for the coming six to twelve months. Compare actual results to your budgeted estimates for each year, and look for areas where you can affect profits with proper controls.

Solution 2: Ask your accountant to suggest analysis procedures that will help you spot trends, predict profits, and meet the goals you have set. Design clear, timely reports that you or your employees can prepare.

Problem 11: Lack of Controls

Description: As your volume of business expands, you notice that expenses are growing at a faster rate than sales. Although the dollar amount of profit is greater, the percentage compared to sales is shrinking.

Solution 1: This is the typical curve that growing small businesses experience. The solution is to put a good deal of effort into a detailed and realistic budget, which you can use as an operating standard. Actual expenses are then measured against the standard and negative trends are identified early. Devise ways (with your accountant's help) to reverse the negative trends.

Solution 2: Establish standards for responsible spending. If you have employees, install an effective but simple approval procedure in advance of spending. If you keep an inventory, lock up smaller, more expensive items. And protect your cash with sound approval and signature procedures.

Problem 12: Building a Bureaucracy

Description: In your effort to control and track transactions, you end up with a lot more paperwork than you want. This cuts into productive time and adds to your expenses.

Solution 1: Systems and controls won't work if they require too much time and paperwork. Design ways to achieve the controls you need while also reducing the burden of the task. Ask your accountant to help design your internal systems.

Solution 2: If you have employees, a bureaucracy will arise when you do not establish standards. Thus it's your responsibility to prevent subordinates from building up the paperwork, systems, or an approval chain that adds to operating expenses. Delegate the task, but be sure you have a say about how efficiently it's done.

Problem 13: Failing to Change

Description: You started your business with a great idea, and your first market thrust was very successful, but now you can see a changing market. Demand is shifting and competitors are cutting into your market share.

Solution 1: Constantly evaluate the state of the market, and be prepared to change your strategy. Those who can't change are left behind. As part of your periodic "quiet time" for planning, study the competitive and demand factors for your product or service, and look for new directions you'll have to take within the coming year.

Solution 2: Keep an open mind to the idea of using unusual marketing tactics, expanding product and service lines, and approaching new markets. Also be aware that what works today could be obsolete next year. Be on constant guard, so that gradual changes don't take you by surprise.

Problem 14: Taking the Wrong Risks

Description: You consider yourself a risk taker and wouldn't have gone into business if you weren't. But now that you've established yourself, one of two changes is taking place: either you have become overly conservative and unwilling to take any risks; or, in the desire to expand, you are attracted to reckless actions.

Solution 1: When you gain experience in managing your business, you might find yourself adopting a more conservative point of view. Be aware that, in order to stay in business, you must continue to take well-planned risks. Evaluate decisions on the basis of risk analysis.

Solution 2: The restless owner who enjoys the chase is constantly looking for the next challenge. Be sure that the attractive risk you're thinking of taking is going to be beneficial to your business, and that it will allow you to maintain profitability.

Problem 15: Inadequate Insurance

Description: Your business has grown to the point that you have greater exposure, in the form of product liability, fire and other casualties, or health of key employees.

Solution 1: Ask for referrals to a qualified commercial insurance broker in your area. Request a review of the policies you have, compared to what you should have. Evaluate each risk in terms of potential economic loss.

Solution 2: Review all business insurance policies no less than twice a year. In an expanding environment, you will have to upgrade your insurance coverage as part of the increased expense of growth.

Problem 16: Leaving Employees Out

Description: During the past year, you have hired several people to handle administrative chores in your service business. With the many responsibilities and pressures you face as owner, you feel that your staff is not involved in developing solutions.

Solution 1: Accept the blame for an uninvolved staff. It's management's job to lead, and that includes getting employees to speak out and contribute. Look for tasks which you do now that could be delegated to others. Ask their advice and opinions, and, most important, when an employee gives you a good suggestion, take it.

Solution 2: Call a weekly, fifteen-minute staff meeting to discuss points of common interest and concern. But don't leave it at the talking stage; give out assignments, delegate, and ask employees to come up with proposals and ideas of their own.

Problem 17: Ignoring Employee Talent

Description: You are faced with the problem of maintaining profits with an expected big push in the market. You fear losing control over the operation, so you're considering hiring a manager from the outside, or even bringing in a consultant.

Solution 1: Before looking outside for help, consider the resources on staff. Gather your employees, express your concerns, and ask them for solutions. Someone might be perfect for the job you're trying to fill.

Solution 2: Whenever you think about hiring a new employee, let your staff know about the opening. Give them first chance at it.

Problem 18: Depending on Consultants

Description: While returning home from a business trip, you strike up a conversation with someone on the plane. He has an office in your area, and specializes in management consulting services. It sounds too good to pass up, and he says he could improve your profits. You're thinking of hiring him.

Solution 1: Before you hire a consultant, determine exactly *how* the person intends to improve conditions in your company. Make sure any agreement is in writing, and that compensation is limited to specific projects, including defined results and a specific time limit.

Solution 2: Ask consultants for a list of their existing clients. Call each and ask how the consultant improved profits or reduced expenses. If the consultant won't give you a list, end the discussion.

Problem 19: Spending Excessively

Description: Your sales volume is growing rapidly. You feel little pressure to control cash outflow because you have more money available now than ever before. But you are also aware that the overhead growth rate is higher than the rate of sales growth.

Solution 1: An alarm bell should go off when the rate of overhead growth exceeds the rate in sales growth. This situation demands immediate management action. Get those expenses down as quickly as possible.

Solution 2: Study the sources of sales growth. Is this new volume as profitable as previous volume? Or are you selling at discounted prices with a lower markup or higher costs? Seek quality volume that increases profits and is controllable; never accept unprofitable volume solely in the interest of expansion.

Problem 20: Failing to Plan Taxes

Description: You've just ended the best year of your company's history. Sales were up more than 30 percent over the last year, and expenses were virtually unchanged. You're elated, at least until your accountant tells you what you owe in taxes.

Solution 1: Meet with your accountant at least twice a year—and well before year-end—to anticipate likely tax liabilities. Ask for advice concerning tax planning. What actions can you take today to reduce taxes? What options are available to you?

Solution 2: Never make a business decision solely to reduce taxes, unless it involves the mere timing of income or expenses. For example, suppose your effective tax rate is 28 percent this year. You are thinking of asking for a loan you don't really need, so that you can write off the interest. Keep in mind that for every $100 you pay in deductible interest, you save only $28 in taxes.

* * *

You face a lot of pressure as a small-business owner, in the sense that you are expected to grow. The ethic states that if you stand still, you're dead. In fact, though, this ethic can be destructive if allowed to rule your decision-making process, or if you let growth occur before you're ready for it. Chapter 2 shows how to deal with and recognize the traps of the expansion ethic.

Notes

1. Kiplinger Washington Editors, *The New American Boom* (Washington, D.C.: Kiplinger, 1986), p. 208.
2. Judith M. Bardwick, *The Plateauing Trap* (New York: AMACOM Books, 1986), p. 103.
3. Roger von Oech, *A Kick in the Seat of the Pants* (New York: Harper & Row, 1986), p. 14.

Chapter 2

The Expansion Ethic

The desire to expand originates with the desire to succeed. Everyone who starts a small business envisions turning that enterprise into an established, profitable, large-volume operation in the future. That objective is entirely appropriate. It was the driving force that created the largest and most powerful organizations that operate today.

If you recognize the importance of expansion as a part of owning and operating your own business, then you also understand the expansion ethic. It's often assumed that growth must continue indefinitely, that the faster the pace the better, and that growth means success. This ethic contains elements of truth. Expansion *is* a positive force, and it is necessary to your operation's health. But when growth becomes the purpose, actually it can ruin a business rather than improve its health.

When you consider the course that failed operations have taken, this becomes evident. Failure often follows a period of rapid growth and diversification. As sales triple or quadruple each year, overhead is increased, often at a greater rate. The company hires employees, leases larger office space, and branches out into new product and service lines. Then, apparently very suddenly, the entire structure falls apart.

It's much less common to see an operation fail because growth has taken place too slowly, or because the owner cut back on expansion. The fact is, a company is at greater risk when growth comes about too quickly, since the owner often loses control over the business, stops contacting customers, and becomes a victim of the expansion ethic.

You probably have already felt the pressure to expand. Undoubtedly you're aware of the way success is judged in the business world. Invariably your "success" hangs on whether or not this year's sales and profits are greater than last year's. But what would happen if you were comfortable with last year's sales? What if you didn't want to expand just yet? Does that mean you're a failure? Of course not.

The common preoccupation with improving past performance is misguided. This expansion ethic may set a standard that's impossible for you to meet, or that jeopardizes your ability to stay in business. Immediate change, or change that takes place too quickly, is *not* healthy for your business, and it doesn't produce long-term growth. You are free to set your own pace, and you have the right to exercise that freedom, regardless of how outsiders judge you. The problem is explained by authors Terrence E. Deal and Allan A. Kennedy:

> The illusion of change has become the quick fix of the business world. Sales are down; reshuffle the marketing department. Operating expenses are too high; install a new budgeting procedure. Market share is slipping; call in the latest consultant to install the newest strategic-planning process. The rent is raised on New York headquarters; move the entire company to the Sun Belt. Change has become such a regular activity in the business world that companies suddenly become suspect if they stay the same.[1]

When small-business owners look to larger companies for their role models, the expansion ethic goes into effect and the pressure for change distorts their perceptions. Rather than following the course they originally conceived for their operations, they feel compelled to change today's profit picture—to rapidly become larger and to seek change for change's sake.

Success in business can be measured not merely by size but by a series of personal standards, each based on the nature of your operation and, perhaps more critically, on your personal motives and objectives. Figure 2-1 and the following list show six areas you can look at to determine the best possible company size and rate of expansion for your business:

1. *Profits.* Your bottom line is the ultimate test of performance. It defines the success of expansion, and it points out the positive or negative results of management and leadership. There is no point in increasing gross volume if profits shrink each year.

2. *Cash Flow.* Many profitable businesses have been forced to close their doors with thousands of dollars in uncollected receivables on the books. Profits on paper are worthless unless the cash is available to keep the operation alive.

Figure 2-1.   Measuring expansion.

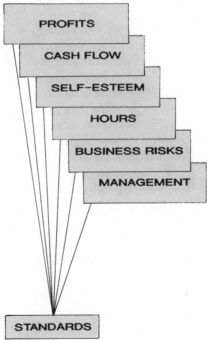

3. *Self-Esteem*. You must have a sense of satisfaction, but this often changes as the result of expansion. If you respond to the demands of staff, vendors, and customers on *their* terms, chances are the expansion ethic has taken over. You no longer control the destiny of your organization; instead, the organization controls you.

4. *Hours*. Are you working longer hours with less profit and less personal reward? And is your staff required to work harder and achieve more in a limited work week? If this is the case, question the value of expansion. It's easy to overlook the importance of a satisfied management and staff when all eyes are focused on greater sales.

5. *Business Risks*. Every business is exposed to a degree of risk and contingent liability. In some respects this risk is offset by insurance; in others, the risk is less tangible or recognizable. For example, when a large company takes on a greater competitive stance, it becomes a target for up-and-coming operations. And expansion demands growth in permanent overhead, which is a profit risk if volume does not keep pace.

6. *Management*. You, either alone or with a team of professional managers, must be able to cope with the day-to-day responsibilities of an expanding company. That means anticipating future problems and dealing with them before they get out of hand; addressing current employee needs for an improved working environment, better benefits, and career advancement; and ensuring quality and customer service. Failing in any of these areas means a decline in reputation, and it increases the chances for serious future problems.

If management of a large organization were easy, two or three very large companies would own all the business interests in the United States. But large corporations have discovered they cannot expand *and* manage indefinitely. So, too, a small business has its own restrictions. Because a small operation is not staffed or financed as well as a large one, there must be special attention to the problems that arise from expansion.

Expanding on Your Own Terms

There are many ways you can achieve profitable expansion, but you have a better chance when it occurs on your terms and not in response to the assumption that you must grow. For example, you can accelerate slightly a previous year's rate of growth and use it as the basis for estimating your volume in the coming year. But this approach ignores several important points that must be remembered in every expansion plan. For example:

1. A business might have already reached the maximum market share it can reasonably expect. Forecasting additional growth from that point is unrealistic. It sets you up for failure.
2. Last year's volume level might be the highest level that can be managed, or that existing capitalization can support. So additional growth will have an adverse effect on quality.
3. Expanding beyond a previous point might require additional facilities, a larger staff, investment in fixed assets, and other major changes. A forecast coordinated with these requirements is most realistic.

The following points, listed in Figure 2-2, should be considered before you attempt to expand:

Figure 2-2.   Conditions for expansion.

1. Expansion must be planned and controlled.

2. Expansion will produce profits.

3. Cash flow will support higher overhead.

4. You can recognize when you've gone too far.

5. The risks are acceptable.

6. You can directly manage growth.

1. *Expansion must be planned and controlled.* Why do you want your business to grow? When expansion is necessary to achieve a specific goal, and within a time limit you set, it is the result of exercising a business plan. But when expansion is forecast as a percentage of last year's volume—on the mere assumption that volume *must* increase each year—it is not a planned occurrence but, rather, an arbitrary and misdirected one.

Misdirected plan example: The president of a regional marketing company prepares a forecast for next year's gross sales. He bases the forecast on several assumptions: that the number of remote regional offices will be expanded, more salespeople will be recruited, and the average salesperson will generate more orders at higher average levels. Obviously all these plans should have limits, however the president assumes only the growth side of the equation, without questioning how realistically the plan can be implemented.

Directed plan example: The president takes a different approach to forecasting next year's sales. He bases the estimates on the previous year's average recruitment of new salespeople, adjusted for turnover. Instead of assuming an increase in average orders placed and size of orders, the forecast assumes the same levels as the previous year. Regional expansion is reduced to a more modest level, based on the number of new offices opened during the previous period.

2. *Expansion will produce profits.* You must be able to afford an expansion program. This might seem obvious, because everyone who forecasts greater future sales also believes the bottom line will reflect a favorable change. But this is not always the case.

For example, a realistic evaluation of a forecast that calls for a 20 percent increase in sales points out the need for other changes. These changes include the need for a larger administrative and sales staff, which also demands larger facilities. It also requires expanding the existing territory, since local competition restricts the potential market. An evaluation should be performed to determine whether the plan is worthwhile. If the added expenses that expansion demand do not offer a respectable profit, is expansion worth the risk? This analysis enables an owner to decide whether a 20 percent growth plan is realistic or whether expansion should be planned at a slower, more methodical rate.

In some instances a business owner is willing to absorb the investment cost of expansion as well as higher overhead for the coming year or two. But this assumes that future profits will justify the profit swing. Losses are acceptable only if they are part of a long-term plan for the development of profits, within a marketing schedule that you can control.

3. *Cash flow will support higher overhead.* One of the great pitfalls for the small-business owner is to seek expansion of sales volume as the solution to today's cash-flow problems—a typical symptom of the expansion ethic. The lack of working capital is a sign of a management problem, not of inadequate volume. Creating a bigger company only multiplies the cash-flow difficulties. What's the solution? To recognize the need for change in the management of cash flow (through inventory control, collection policies for receivables, and timing of expense payments, for example), and then deal with the issue of volume expansion separately.

4. *You* can *recognize when you've gone too far.* One form of expansion calls for taking a step backward. Many companies have expanded to the point at which overhead is unreasonably high, they are overstaffed or top-heavy, and their profits are down. The owners recall the "good old days," when greater profits were earned on a lower volume.

It might not be too late to turn back. As an alternative to losing money as a consequence of growth, why not lay off some employees, lease a smaller office or shop, and reduce sales volume? Simplifying your operation is often the most obvious, logical solution. Reduction of scope is not a sign of failure; it could be the best way to produce a profit and stay in business. Expansion can wait until you are ready.

A small business owner might say, "I want a bigger operation" without accepting the reality of this situation. Examine your reasons for setting a standard based only on the size of your company. It makes sense to plan expansion as a methodical, controlled process, rather than try to make your sales statistics go off the chart in one or two years. Achieving growth because you want it is a positive goal, but only assuming you can direct and control its rate.

5. *The risks are acceptable.* The stakes increase whenever a company raises its volume. Expansion can't be perceived just as a condition of greater sales and profits, because many risk factors come into the growth equation. If you deal with the public, expansion means broadening your exposure to public liability, necessitating higher insurance premiums and the risk that some form of contingent loss will not be covered under your business insurance policy. A larger company also assumes a more visible competitive posture, requiring a shift to the defensive. There are always plenty of smaller operations that want part of your market share; the bigger your company becomes, the more vulnerable it is. Finally, growth is accompanied by the inevitable creation of permanent overhead. Chances are, higher volume will be translated into more dollars in profit, but with a lower return on sales. You must determine whether the risks and complications of rapid expansion are worth that change.

6. *You can directly manage growth.* Your ability to directly control growth determines whether the growth is permanent and profitable or temporary and costly. When growth occurs too rapidly, you lose control. In a planned growth situation, you—either directly or through a capable management team— need to anticipate needs for greater planning and monitoring of costs and expenses, to ensure that profits and cash flow will not deteriorate as sales volume grows.

The Realistic Review

In corporations, employees are reviewed by a supervisor and given exact guidelines for improving their performance. But when you own your own business, your only source of dependable review is yourself. You may easily miss what's obvious to everyone else: Growth for its own sake will ruin an efficient, responsive, and profitable operation. If growth itself is the goal, you're a victim of the expansion ethic. Don't respond to the idea that you must grow. Instead, listen to your own advice, expressed in your personal and business goals.

Here is a three-part exercise for evaluating your rate of business growth:

1. *List the reasons you had for starting your own business as you perceived them before opening your doors.* Include these points:

- To set your own course
- To escape corporate bureaucracy
- To apply creative ideas and energy
- To be in charge
- To earn more money

Chances are, you did not want to start your own business to reduce your hours. Or if you did, you soon discovered that running your own business means putting in even more hours. It's more likely that you are driven by your business, and that it's your primary life interest. The key, though, is to recognize emerging problems and then to take steps to control the time you spend.

2. *List the status of your business today, compared to each of the points you listed in step 1.* Ask yourself these questions:

- Are you following the course you wanted? You might find yourself heading in a direction you never antici- pated. It might not be where you want your business to go.

Example: An entrepreneur saw an opportunity to start a mail order business. She invested money, created a catalog, and began operating. After a few months, she expanded her operation by opening a retail outlet for her merchandise, and then another. But upon review, she found that her retail stores were losing money and creating numerous headaches. The original plan was to operate a simple, low-overhead, low-risk mail order enterprise. The obvious course: to get out of the retail store business.

- Have you escaped bureaucracy and politics? As your business expands, you might find yourself creating the same situation, or a worse one, that you suffered as an employee.

Example: An engineer broke away from his corporate job, where he spent most of his time on budgets, employee problems, and administration. Several years later, he was back in the same position, but now he was president and the bureaucracy was worse than ever. The obvious course: to get back to the more simplified business he'd envisioned.

- Are you using your creative energy, or have the risks of running your own show made you conservative and conventional?

Example: A young woman left her company to open a fashion boutique, with the idea of merchandising unusual designs. But after several years in business, she realized that her stock was conventional and that she was not taking the risks she'd originally wanted to take. The obvious course: to recognize the source of her unhappiness, and make changes in the way she organizes her stores and selects her merchandise.

- Are you truly in charge, or do the demands of your operation dictate where your time and energy are spent? If you're not able to control your own activity and time, then you must ask yourself why you are living with the risks and responsibilities of "independence." You need to make specific and immediate changes so that you are again in charge of your daily routine.

Example: An architect had never found satisfaction working for someone else. He thought he had a better management idea. But now, with his business expanded to a $.5 million a year, he spent his time solving problems for employees, meeting deadlines, and handling administrative crises. The obvious course: to face the issue by examining the volume, delegation process, nature of work, and staff priorities in his service. He reminded himself of his own priorities, and then took action to position himself where he wanted to be.

3. *Where do you want to go? Will you achieve the goals you set for yourself when you get there? If not, it's time to reexamine your decisions.* List the steps you need to take today to get back on course. If your original objective is still relevant, identify the steps you've taken that led you off course, and reverse that direction. Only then will expansion become a positive form of change, and only then will you be able to expand on *your* terms.

Examining and questioning allows you to control expansion on your own terms. And when you discover you've made a mistake, undo the damage, even if that means reducing the size of your company until you're ready to put expansion into action.

Taking Positive Action

If a review leads you to the conclusion that your business has expanded in the wrong direction, or that current plans are misdirected, you must take action. Follow the guidelines listed here and in Figure 2-3.

1. *Admit the error.* There is no flaw in being error-prone. The flaw develops when you fail to take action to make a

Figure 2-3.   Redirection: taking positive action.

1. Admit the error.

2. Specify and eliminate the problem.

3. Throw out your old plan and budget.

4. Abandon misdirected thinking.

positive change. But before that can occur, you must be willing to accept responsibility.

2. *Specify and eliminate the problem.* Admitting there is a problem does not tell you how to fix it. To find that, you must list the specific errors and then make corrections. Here are some examples:

- You have been pursuing the wrong kind of volume. Don't allow yourself to think you're stuck with it. Get rid of the business that doesn't produce a profit.
- Some of your customers pay slowly and give you the greatest headaches. Stop working with them; put your energy into more positive avenues.
- Operating expenses have grown well beyond what you consider a reasonable level. Take immediate steps to cut back. Institute approval procedures, if you have employees; question every invoice; shop around for better prices; develop a budget and use it to hold expenses down.
- You have hired the wrong people for the job. If the ratio between management and employees is too great—if you have more people on the payroll than you need, or if there are no real controls over hiring—make the changes you need to survive. If necessary, lay off excessive staff.
- You are competing in the wrong way. You can't afford to play by rules set by larger, deeper-entrenched, and better-financed competitors. Look for marketing opportunities that work around the established competitors. Set your own rules.

3. *Throw out your old plan and budget.* There is no point following a plan that's moving you in the wrong direction, based on the wrong assumptions and designed to achieve the wrong objectives. Start from scratch. Keep your original objectives in mind, and simplify what you want to achieve in the near future.

4. *Abandon misdirected thinking.* If you find yourself saying, "I can't" or "I should," it's time to examine your thinking

process. As the owner of a small business you *can* and *will* achieve what you want. If you have become more conservative now that you've been in business for a while, take a good look at what you want and how you must operate in order to achieve it.

Recognizing Valid Growth

Don't confuse reversing a misdirected course with failure. To recognize healthy, well-directed growth, you need to review and monitor standards (see Figure 2-4). This is perhaps the most critical function you perform as an owner or manager of a small business. Here are some guidelines:

1. *Always refer to the original plan.* When you opened your business, you created an agenda for yourself. It might have been written down, or it might have been only in your head. In either case, it's time to list your objectives again.

If you have changed your mind, and have moved away from your original idea, write down what you want to achieve now. But if your original purpose still holds true today, that's the best guideline for keeping yourself on the right track.

Example: A consultant set up shop to work for several clients, with the objective of controlling his own time. But after five years in

Figure 2-4.   Guidelines: review standards.

1. **Always refer to the original plan.**

2. **Seek growth that is personally satisfying.**

3. **Seek profitable volume.**

4. **Seek permanent growth.**

the business, he had only one major client and he spent most of his time at that company's offices. Once he realized he was functioning much like an employee, he knew it was time for a change. He sought and won several smaller contracts, and he returned to the original plan of diversifying his income dependence.

2. *Seek growth that is personally satisfying.* Accomplishment and achievement are addictive to the owner of a small business; it's natural to continually seek more rewards and to expand. You can't go wrong, however, as long as the rate of expansion and the level you achieve are satisfying to you.

Example: An editor left his job at a large national publisher to start his own small press. For the first few years, he produced a limited number of books and, with careful market research, made a decent profit. But with expansion, he began losing money on larger book contracts. He realized that the compulsion to expand had taken him away from his original plan.

3. *Seek profitable volume.* Increased volume is a positive sign only when it also creates profit. Some forms of business have a high cost and expense factor, and they demand greater activity to produce desired results. That higher volume translates to greater complications.

Example: The president of an advertising firm opened branch offices in one state only, and made a decent profit each year. But in expanding, he developed into remote areas. The resulting higher cost of travel, administrative control, and home office staffing made these ventures less profitable. The president realized the error in attempting to expand too rapidly, and he closed the remote offices. This resulted in higher profits the following year.

4. *Seek permanent growth.* It's easy to mistake a one-time spurt in volume, or even a seasonal change, for permanent growth. Real growth is recognized by its permanent nature, in terms of both the money you bring in and the money you have to pay out to operate your business. The mistake that often occurs is in allowing permanent overhead to grow while permanent sales growth stays the same.

Example: A commercial artist operated from her home and without employees for three years. Then, within three months, she won several large contracts. She signed a lease for office space and hired a receptionist. But once the new contracts were completed, the volume of business decreased to near its previous level and was not adequate to support the rent and salary expense she had added.

Ways of Expanding

Your judgment of "quality" growth is affected by the type of expansion you experience. The expansion ethic usually deals only with growth in sales volume, but this is just the most obvious form. There are many other forms of expansion, each of which presents its own opportunities, dangers, and expansion ethic matters, such as:

1. *New product or service lines.* Large companies don't compete only by developing their own goods and services; often they acquire small competitors and eliminate them by absorption. Small-business owners can't afford to buy out competitors, but they may want to expand by diversifying their range of sales. But if you are tempted to expand product or service lines, first ask yourself how much of that desire is driven by the expansion ethic, and how much is good business sense?

2. *Geographic influence.* Many entrepreneurs are content only while their businesses are in the formative stages. Once they settle down and run as a business, the entrepreneurs lose interest. A common response is to seek expansion by opening more shops or offices—to continue in an entrepreneurial vein. But when the motive is to gain competitive power and influence, expansion is a trap for young businesses. Owners must first map out a geographic growth plan and determine how it will be financed over time, with cash-flow requirements a major consideration. Unfortunately the entrepreneurial spirit is not always in harmony with the demands of business management.

3. *Facilities and assets.* Some business owners believe they are successful if they lease larger space this year than the year

before, and they invest in more equipment, machinery, and furniture. But these forms of expansion must occur as a necessary phase of well-planned expansion. When you invest in facilities and capital assets in *anticipation* of future growth, the expansion process is executed in reverse.

4. *Employee expansion.* Staff increases are difficult to time. Don't hire people you don't need today. In too many cases, an owner recruits executives, managers, or employees so that growth—if and when it occurs—can be managed. Or the owner hires on the assumption that the "right people" will somehow create growth. But expansion of employees must be budgeted in a well-controlled marketing plan, and must be coordinated with a gradual increase in sales volume, customers, and support systems.

5. *Overhead.* You can't measure growth accurately by reviewing the level of overhead. Yet many owners believe that doubling their operating expenses is the same as a positive expansion of their business. The correct way to measure growth is by tracking profits. Only with greater volume and a controlled, stable level of operating expenses is the bottom line improved. When overhead grows at or above sales, it has a deteriorating effect on the entire operation.

6. *Competitive posture.* Becoming the major supplier of goods and services in a defined territory is certainly one sign of permanent, profitable expansion. However, this form of growth should be the result of careful and well-directed management, not the purpose itself. You might aim for this as a specific goal, but chances are, without the needed timing and control procedures, an advantageous competitive posture will be impossible to achieve. The need to actively manage is inevitable, and the owner needs to manage at a higher level than any employee.

*   *   *

The expansion traps that every small business encounters as it begin to grow are examined in detail in Part 2. The next chapter is concerned with the need for a focused business objective: the original premise that inspired a small-business owner to break away from the company and strike out in a new direction.

Note

1. Terrence E. Deal and Allan A. Kennedy, *Corporate Cultures* (Reading, Mass.: Addison-Wesley, 1982), p. 157.

Chapter 3

Focusing Your Objectives

What is your business objective? The answer to this question may seem obvious to anyone who has taken the time to define a market, product, or service and obtain the necessary capital structure for getting an operation up and running. Yet many business owners do not know how to respond; among those who do have an answer, a fair analysis of their response might reveal that it isn't really an objective at all.

The word *objective* is used loosely in business. Unfortunately, everyone has his or her own definition of the concept, what use it serves in operating successfully, and how (or if) it is to be implemented. In the context of this book, an objective gives a primary theme and purpose to a business. It is specific and addresses the primary individuals or groups with whom a business owner must deal: customers, employees, and vendors. In some companies, notably those subject to strict regulation and oversight, the regulatory agencies involved should also be addressed in the objective. Thus the purpose of an objective is to guide a company's owner and its employees toward a well-understood standard.

Many organizations have attempted to define their objectives without achieving agreement among those who must operate within it. Remember that for the objective to work it must be more than just a token statement; it must be put into practice. Also remember that just because the objective is in writing, it does not mean employees will adhere to it. Owners need to make sure that their objective goes into action.

The Attributes of Success

An objective keeps a business on course. Once you begin to concentrate on day-to-day operations, it's easy to lose sight of *why* you went into business in the first place. The allure of starting a new business is not financial; it's the satisfaction of putting an idea into effect, of expressing your creativity, and of finding a responsive market for your product or service. You will probably agree that an objective must reflect your own perception of success. Yet even the idea of what makes someone successful is difficult to define.

For example, the owner of a five-store retail establishment started with no outside capital; he built up the business using his personal savings. For a while, he barely held on, staying only one step ahead of the bills. But seven years later his operation was running profitably, cash flow was no problem, and the business was growing at an amazing rate. Most significantly, he was still in control of the expansion. His objective was working.

At about this time, though, this owner received a buyout offer that would make him modestly wealthy. The owner's perception of success involved applying his own creative energy, remaining independent, and expanding in a profitable, planned manner. Now the prospect of realizing a huge profit confused the issue. Should he stick to his original idea or take the money? Does "success" mean reaching the ultimate financial goal, or allowing the existing program to continue? And if he did take the money and give up control, what would he do next?

To an employee on a fixed, limited income, the choice might seem obvious: Money would solve a lot of problems and might even be assumed to be what the owner was aiming at all along. But to the owner of a small and growing business, the objective of *creating* a business might be of greater importance, even seven years later. Having taken the risks, overcome them, and gained the freedom to run the show his own way, why should he throw it all away?

How does an individual define success? Owners who determine the personal priorities that drive them will arrive at a clear understanding of what success means to them. And this helps to clarify objectives—at the onset of an enterprise, during its expansion, and at future growth plateaus.

For example, many business objectives contain the word *excellence*. The word is applied to customer service and vaguely refers to quality, product development, or recruitment of an internal staff. But *excellence*—like the word *objective*—can have different meanings. If you describe excellence for your company in terms of what constitutes success, you will soon reach the same conclusion. Excellence defines success, which then defines your objective—whether you seek profits, personal satisfaction, social benefits, employee motivation and response, customer loyalty, or competitive leadership.

Constructive change, which happens when you meet your objective, may occur internally or externally. Internal change includes staff development and response; external change is seen in competitive posture and increased customer loyalty, for example. No matter how you define excellence, the important point is that if you concentrate your objective on achieving the positive attributes of the business you want to lead, you are on the track that leads to success.

Expansion must not be discouraged solely in the interest of staying small. You can expand without losing the qualities of excellence as you desire it. Author and management expert Robert Townsend observes:

> Please pursue excellence—not growth. If it leads to flat spots in your sales and profits curve, so be it. Who says human beings or human organizations don't need breathing spells?
>
> If everyone in your company and all your customers know that your goal is excellence, then you've done your job. Keep on doing it and take

what comes. Let everybody enjoy being part of the best even if it's not the biggest.[1]

Company presidents all promptly insist that excellence is a central, basic theme of their business—the one that guides their objective. Yet every consumer knows that many businesses are not operated with the goal of excellence. Lip service or commitment to a vague notion of excellence (or quality, or success, or profits) will not lead to success. Likewise, the vague notion of excellence is often obscured, lost in the rush toward greater volume.

The commitment to excellence must be defined with specific, achievable attributes, not limited to brief mention in the objective statement. This way you can monitor it and weigh its importance vis-à-vis expansion. For example, a food manufacturer made a commitment to developing a product from home recipes. But expansion to a certain level would mean giving up its commitment to personal care. In another example, a professional defined *excellence* as his personal involvement with each client. This would have to be compromised, and perhaps lost, if expansion necessitated eliminating the direct contact he so highly valued.

Expansion through delegation or enhanced efficiency does not always mean that an original version of excellence must be sacrificed. But in the expansion process the changes must be accompanied with improved control procedures, lest the idea of excellence become vague and the attribute that made the business excellent be lost to volume and administrative concerns. When that occurs, profits will eventually erode, and some other smaller and more motivated entrepreneur will come along and take away the market.

To avoid this, you can avoid expansion completely, even when that means giving up profit opportunities. Alternatively, the objective that guides you can be kept intact, even when the scope of business changes drastically. Perhaps the best alternative is to accept expansion as a natural course of events but to create controls that ensure excellence is not lost.

Examples of Business Objectives

To construct your own statement of objectives, decide exactly what standards you want your operation to follow. Are you striving for exceptional customer service, quality products, or some other attribute that sets your company apart from—and makes it better than—the competition? In writing the statement, remember that it must be clear and simple so there is no doubt about what you want or how you will achieve it. Everyone should know at once what standards you apply to yourself and to those who work for you. For example, here are some statements to help show how it should and should not be written:

Vague: "The Midtown Consulting Group offers excellent service to its customers, and specializes in general business consultation."

Specific: "Midtown Consulting Group ensures personal attention to every customer and operates from the standard that the customer will profit from retaining our services. This is achieved through recruitment of only the most capable professionals with track records of successful consultation experience."

*   *   *

Vague: "Automated Bookkeeping offers fast and accurate bookkeeping services to small companies, and also provides management consulting when needed."

Specific: "Automated Bookkeeping serves the small-business customer requiring prompt, professional, and accurate service. Our purpose is to provide consultation and bookkeeping services at the level the customer needs."

*   *   *

Vague:	"Hodges Associates does graphic design work for a variety of clients, and tries to keep the cost of services down to a reasonable level."
Specific:	"Hodges Associates offers high-quality, individualized graphic design services at a reasonable cost. Our purpose is not to become the largest design service in the city, but to satisfy the client's needs in every case."

*   *   *

Vague:	"Financial Alternatives is a full-service broker-dealer with a national sales force and an experienced staff. We offer a wide variety of investment product and services."
Specific:	"Financial Alternatives is a national brokerage firm that recruits experienced and professional representatives, to offer tested and proven, high-quality products to the general public. Compliance with regulation is ensured through the recruitment of an experienced internal staff, whose purpose is to ensure continued excellence in sales support, product quality, and reporting."

Defining Your Objective

An objective should represent the primary purpose and standard of your company (see Figure 3-1). A clearly defined objective can be expressed in one or two sentences, to describe the purpose of the business, the product or service offered, and the standards by which it operates.

1. *Purpose.* This is the driving force or philosophy that led you to start the business. Most new business owners are

Figure 3-1. Elements of the objective.

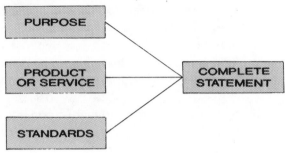

strong-willed and determined people with a belief system that leads, inevitably, to independence in a career. For example, the entrepreneur is willing to take risks, believing that the rewards will more than offset them. A frustrated employee might believe, "I can manufacture this product at a lower price, and make more money, too." The professional might believe he or she has enough experience and contacts to break away and open a new firm. And many businesses are started with strong social ideals and a purpose—perhaps to create a participative environment in which employees feel free to speak openly with top management.

2. *Product or Service.* Beyond your own belief system is a primary product or range of products, or there is a service for which you have perceived a market. When the in-demand product or service is combined with your business philosophy, the organization assumes a central, unifying character. The objective defines the ideal business character you want to achieve, and also how the company must operate to remain true to that character.

3. *Standards.* The objective includes a commitment to product or service excellence (such as customer satisfaction, quality, and responsiveness). Many new owners fail to define their young company's primary objective, which means that they are not able to readily explain to vendors, customers, or employees why their company exists or what it wants to achieve.

If we were to ask the managers of a *large* company to write down their company's objectives, we'd probably get as many answers as there are individuals in the survey. For example, the vice-president of a life insurance company was promoted to the president/CEO spot. His first action was to call together the company's executives and middle managers. He told each one, "Write down, in fifty words or less, the primary objective of this organization." When everyone had finished writing, he collected the responses, mixed them up, and read them one by one. The answers were diverse. They included:

To sell life insurance at a profit
To assist the public in protecting their families
To invest reserves to produce profits that exceed costs and expenses
To gain a larger market share than our competitors

As you can see, everyone had a different point of view about what the company stood for. This exercise identified the need to carefully examine and define the business a company is in, the purpose it serves, and the basic standards under which it operates.

> As long as a single, specific objective has not been expressed, the company cannot work toward the common purpose—because no one knows what it is.

If you and your employees see the operation from different points of view, you will not work together on any level, because there is no unifying, understood purpose.

For example, a securities marketing company sold investments through a series of independent offices. The company provided regulatory, licensing, and oversight and processed commission statements. When the owner tried to formulate an objective, he discovered that several points of view were in effect:

- The compliance officer believed the company existed to police field personnel.

- The marketing director thought the company's purpose was to sell directly to the public.
- The sales manager saw the home office as a service group to support field offices.

None of the perceptions was complete, although each contributed to what the company represented. Even the most basic question—*Who is the customer?*—had not been answered. In one respect, the general public was the customer; in another, it was field offices. The owner needed to resolve the different points of view before a valid objective could be constructed and published.

Creating an objective statement is the essential first step for well-controlled growth. Without agreement as to what the company hopes to achieve, there can be no valid plan, since everyone must operate on assumption. But once you and your employees agree on what the business is all about, everyone at least is aimed in the same direction.

This is not mere theory. It is necessary in formulating the most important questions a company must answer, including:

- Who is the customer, and how do we serve the market?
- How much expansion is desirable, how quickly, and in which directions?
- How will our *planned* expansion affect profits? What are the pitfalls, and what can we do now to avoid them?
- Must we change our product or service lines, our market thrust, or our competitive posture in the future? And how will those changes affect our ability to expand?

The objective is the foundation of the plan and the basis of the planning process. But the statement you write is not the objective; it's only the expression of your standards. Given the energy that goes into developing a twenty-five- or fifty-word definition, it's easy to think the job ends there. In fact, it's only the beginning.

The MBO Theory

Among the scores of management theories that have been described in books and articles over the last twenty years, one of the best-known is Management by Objective (MBO). This is a rather simple idea that often becomes too complex and is given too many attributes.

In theory, MBO unifies your company under a single purpose, or objective. But by itself a statement cannot create a team. It only lays the groundwork for the task ahead. Once the objective has been defined—often the most elusive phase of the MBO program—the team then devises the tangible, specific action steps needed to put the philosophy into practice. This involves both formulating a strategic plan and following strategic management.

There is a difference between a strategic plan and strategic management. The plan is the idea for making your operation work, dividing internal resources, and approaching the competition. Strategic management is getting the idea off the table and into the field. To do the latter, you need controls, budgets and forecasts, and marketing programs—all aimed at achieving the stated objective.

Many companies that acknowledge the value of MBO nevertheless fail in bridging the gap between objectives and plans. They may spend a great deal of time developing an objective statement but then do not take it any further. Daniel H. Gray, president and CEO of a strategic management consulting firm based in Boston, collected over 500 responses from planning directors and CEOs through a questionnaire and during a seminar. He found that:

> Approximately seven out of ten companies in our sample do not carry the formulation of strategy much beyond some general statement of thrust such as market penetration or internal efficiency and some generalized goal such as excellence. Having only generalizations to work with makes implementation very difficult. Targets don't mean much if no one maps out the pathways leading to them.[2]

Three Common Situations

You really have three choices: (1) to run your business without any clear objectives, (2) to establish the right objectives as you currently perceive them, or (3) to remain with a defined objective that is now wrong for you and your company. You might find yourself in any or all of these situations at different times in the life of your business.

Growth Without Objectives

Your company may expand even when you don't operate within the confines of a primary objective. However, that exposes you to the very risks that threaten your company's ability to survive. The lack of a plan (and an objective) means that if growth occurs at all, it will be arbitrary and undirected. If it takes place too rapidly for your employees to administer, if it moves you into new markets you can't service, or if it places excessive demand on working capital, then you risk failure.

Many entrepreneurs think that self-confidence, enthusiasm, and belief in ideals are an adequate substitute for a sensible plan. They hold the planning process in low regard because it smacks of the big-company bureaucracy, attitude, and approach they tried to escape. But there is a difference between ineffective objectives that *sound* like MBO and the simple, logical practice of MBO. The objective specifies the course, and the plan is the blueprint for implementation. The importance of the plan is explained by business writer Ronaleen R. Roha.

> Running a business by the seat of your pants rather than according to a written plan is the surest killer of all. Bankers and outside investors will insist on inspecting your plan, but even if you don't need outside capital, a plan serves to sharpen your focus by charting a realistic course through the blinding glare of enthusiasm.[3]

Taking a nonplanning approach is, indeed, a major cause of failure among small businesses. Just as the avenues for expansion open up the owner loses control and everything falls apart. This failure is given many names—lack of capital, strong competition, poor market response, or no employee loyalty, for example—but it all comes down to a *lack* of objective and the inability to create a working plan.

Growth With the Right Objectives

Causing your company to grow—and not just accepting growth by chance—is the obvious right solution. The problems confronted by the nonplanning manager don't occur, while other problems are easily overcome. But this requires an honest evaluation of the basic questions every owner should ask, again and again:

- What business am I in?
- Who is my customer?
- What are my personal expectations, and how can they be fulfilled through this business?
- What operating standards must I apply to remain true to myself?

Once you establish a clear objective and gain consensus, your team might take it over and run with it—to the degree that your role is reduced to Management by Exception, an alternative to MBO. This is possible and efficient, since it frees up your time so you can act as the executive you should be. But in any growing company, this situation develops only *after* a period of well-directed expansion. Once the profitable operation of your business is established, and the objective is at work to guide the company, you can best serve as troubleshooter.

The "right" objective for each phase might not be all that easy to define. You may find that you have two different objectives in conflict with one another. For example, the reasons for starting your own business may have been to (1) escape the big-company restriction on your creativity and independence, and (2) make a lot of money. Once you begin operating, though, you may conclude that staying at a manageable level restricts your potential income—a conflict between your two objectives.

A second problem arises when you consult a management team within your company. Different people will perceive the purpose and objective of your company in dissimilar ways. Each may hold valid and important priorities, but they might not be reconcilable. This situation demands a tough decision from the top. For example, the sales manager encourages you to pursue a course of significant expansion. The argument makes sense, and the opportunity is there. However, the administrative team points out that you do not have the support staff, the computer system, or the inventory to afford expansion. You will require an infusion of capital if expansion is to succeed. Both sides cannot be pleased, and you do not want to give up equity or borrow money. The final decision should be made on the basis of the right objectives, for you and for your company.

Some "right" objectives are easily stated and defined, but they prove difficult to put into practice. For example, part of your objective might be to provide "the highest quality" service to your customers. In practice, achieving this could be your greatest management challenge. For example, you have the opportunity to grow rapidly because no one else is taking advantage of a specific market demand. If your objective includes the desire to provide quality service, how can you achieve growth and still remain responsive to market demand? The answer: You need to reconcile the desire for maintaining quality, with the opportunity for rapid growth. You will discover that a gradual, controlled course will be necessary in order to achieve growth and the objective at the same time.

Growth With the Wrong Objectives

Today's "right" objective might change next year—or even next week. As a general rule, the big-picture ideals remain the same in the long term, but as competition, demand, cost, and capital factors change, so might your more immediate objectives. If you find unexpected good fortune, and your company could become more profitable than you dared dream, that presents a challenge. Do you stick to your original objective for simplicity and direct control, or do you become another large company with a wealthy owner and an expensive internal bureaucracy?

Expansion itself can make your original objective invalid. If you conclude that, in order to remain in business, you *must* grow, but that growth means giving up your original objective, then you must make a decision. At this point many owners lose control of their companies. They either hold onto their original idea but encourage growth (meaning they impede control during periods of growth, becoming the source of the problem); or they give up direct control to a team of outside managers and end up as a part of the big company—just as they were before breaking away.

Expansion is not the only factor that can make yesterday's objective the wrong one today. Change is constant, even when business is stable and restricted. The developing maturity of the owner, the staff, and the market all characterize change. It's even fair to say that when an operation's environment *doesn't* change in some way, the business stagnates.

Thus defining an objective and putting it into effect does not end the process. Operating via an objective is a continuing management task, one which must be modified and updated with time. What was on the mark a few months ago could be in left field today. So, the objective itself must develop and expand as the company matures and finds its market. The allure of freedom is not lost as a company changes its nature. Focusing on a new idea and being able to create a company to bring it to market is the initial phase; being able to change over time is the real test of your talent.

With that in mind, it is apparent that an original objective will invariably change, even when the idea holds true in a new environment. For example, a food manufacturer might start out with one product and the premise that a specific, personalized recipe will find a market. A few years later, that standard might still apply to a broader range of food products, however the objective must be expanded (not necessarily changed) to remain valid in the larger environment.

Often, successful completion of an expansion is itself the source of a new objective. Expansion changes an owner's perspective, and presents a new range of challenges and problems to be overcome. For example, a personnel manager started her own consulting firm, working with medium-size employers. She helped companies write employee manuals, develop internal policies, and build evaluation and review procedures. After two years she found that her clients needed the systems at the onset of the relationship, but that after this phase they wanted ongoing consultation even more. She ultimately hired others to help with the building of documents, and devoted her time to backup services. Her original idea had taken on a new character; rather than providing a tangible product, she became a resource for management as well as for line employees.

Retaining Your Objectives

Because timely, profitable expansion is a positive form of change, it is inaccurate to claim that smaller is always better. Smaller may be more manageable, but it is often less profitable. Ultimately, you must determine whether expansion fits with your objective. And that's not reason enough in every case.

For example, suppose your original objective was to provide highly personalized services to a limited number of customers. When you started your business, you thought you would always work alone, thus achieving your objective was a matter of individual control. But now that your business has expanded, you have three other people on the payroll, and you expect them to conform to your standards. In this case, you must ask yourself:

1. *Can I deliver the same degree of service when other people are involved?* You might conclude that you can't offer personalized service when you're not seeing clients yourself. But the objective can be altered to allow for expansion without giving up the commitment to quality.

2. *How can I enforce the standard?* It is possible to delegate work to others, but it is much tougher to ensure that they approach work with the same diligence that you do. Enforcement demands constant monitoring, reminding, and checking.

3. *How much more growth can I expect, without having to abandon the personalized service ideal?* This is the critical question. Indeed, there is a natural conflict between expansion and personalized service. Do you want to stay small and offer personalized service? Or do you want your business to grow, and replace "personalized" service with the highest "quality" service? And exactly what does that mean to you? How will you successfully compete with other companies of the same size?

In confronting these issues you will realize that expansion changes your objective and that today's objective, if followed, may inhibit the expansion that you need and want. Once you have questioned the validity of your objective, you must next ask three questions concerning your approach to expansion:

1. *When should expansion occur, and at what pace? How do the company's objectives restrict the pace of expansion?* For example, an employee of a large software manufacturing firm left to start his own consulting business. Demand for his services was high, and the opportunity to expand gross volume was apparent. Considering limitations of capital and the desire to offer highly personalized service, the owner had to decide how much expansion was possible—without violating the objective.

2. *Is expansion inevitable and unavoidable, based on the objective?* For example, the owner of a small manufacturing concern was faced with a problem. Higher volume of production meant lower direct costs, thus potentially greater profits. She concluded that it would be impossible to compete with larger-volume competitors, since her prices continued to rise with low volume. Expansion was unavoidable.

3. *Is expansion controllable?* For example, a contractor specialized in working very closely with homeowners, building custom homes with the finest materials and workmanship. He was offered an opportunity to win a contract for a new, very large development. He needed to decide whether the new project could be built to the same standard he applied to smaller jobs. To what degree would quality-control standards

prevent or curtail permanent growth? If rapid growth is possible only with a compromise in quality, then it isn't healthy expansion.

You might determine that expansion, although not desirable, is unavoidable. In this case, you must ask yourself whether the newly expanded environment will place a demand on your management skills, or on the level of hands-on management you're willing to exercise. This must be related to staff and their morale; to the geographic territory your business serves; and to the strength of your competition for the same business.

Example: The owner of an engineering consultation firm knew that he must allow growth to occur, since the types of contracts he was winning required greater staffing than he currently retained. He feared that internal paperwork and control systems would stifle the present informal work environment. To reconcile these opposing demands, the owner needed to study realistically the changes that might occur. Without personal attention, leadership, and enforcement of the objective, he feared that power struggles and internal conflicts would corrupt the smoothly running operation. The bureaucracy would strangle creativity. And paperwork would become the company's primary product. The owner, in dealing with expansion, needed to determine whether to allow the trend to take its own course and merely to follow, or to prevent the negative changes and truly to lead the process. He solved the problem by hiring a full-time office manager and delegating administrative responsibility within the guidelines of the company's objective.

In some instances you might be compelled to simply abandon your objectives. Flexibility is essential. Remember that in the exciting environment of the small company, change is constant. The objective is important only in that it keeps a company on course. But what must occur when that course is altered by outside factors? And when is abandoning an objective simply realism, as opposed to just selling out?

Consider what can occur to an original objective in the following situations:

- An existing, strong competitor leaves the field, opening up new opportunities to expand.

- A new, well-financed competitor enters the field and begins eroding your market share.
- Marketing strategies, product or service lines, or customer demands change owing to obsolescence.
- An offer comes in to take the company public, and go from a regional concern to a national one.

These are but a few of the possible events that could drastically change the way your business operates. You might find yourself thinking back to the old days, when the business environment was truly entrepreneurial, when the creative outlets were everywhere, and when a small and informal staff had to work long hours for every penny of profit, but worked together with a sense of commitment and excitement. But the old days are gone, and you can't go back.

What might be though of as "success" for a small business could ultimately destroy your reasons for starting it in the first place. When your personal satisfaction is gone, and when the original objective becomes lost in the complications of a newly evolved big business, what is the benefit of expansion?

Resisting Growth

Any form of change is disruptive, and it must be expected to bring negative as well as positive consequences. Hidden beneath many "success stories" is the personal misery of an overwhelmed owner, who asserted a nonconforming spirit and turned his back on the establishment—only to go full circle and end up back in the middle of it all. Once strongly focused, the owner is now lost and without direction. The illusion of success is shattered when expansion robs the entrepreneur of the freedom and independence he worked so hard to achieve.

Should you fight change? Is staying small a benefit? And is it realistic to believe that demand can be ignored? Fame and fortune are very tempting—almost impossible to resist. If your business takes off—in spite of your relatively modest personal objectives—you might find yourself unable to stop the expanding role you will have to play. For the renegade, it's certainly demoralizing to look in the mirror and see the type of boss you used to work for—and hated.

On the other hand, you can control how much you have to give up. The rate of expansion, the amount of outside capital you let in, and even whether or not you become a big-time operation are all up to you. If you want, you can choose principle over financial success, and expand at your own rate and on your own terms.

This alternative does present problems, however. For example, suppose you have the opportunity to expand because your business is in an excellent competitive position. If you don't take advantage of the situation now, other companies will certainly fill the gap. It might come down to a question of *who* will expand—you or someone else. If you don't act now, will your competitors take away your entire market? Must you remain market leader, or can you stay small, profitable, *and* in control—without threatening your business health?

No matter what objectives you have set, unexpected demand and expansion opportunities can cloud your judgment and blur your focus. Most owners and managers live with the general assumption that expansion is always good. This is the expansion ethic, which was discussed in Chapter 2. You must be able to question this ethic:

> If it's possible to allow unexpected growth to occur, that also means you can expand at a slower, more controlled rate and on your own terms.

Given that all circumstances are different, this does not always mean that staying in direct control is an entirely advantageous decision. To stick to your principles, you might have to give up a controlling position, lost part of your market share, or allow someone else to take the glory of going national.

Rapid growth is applauded in the business press and held in awe by most business people. Owners whose companies expand within the first few years become the mentors and role models for every new business. And when your company succeeds in terms of size and market scope, there is a general assumption that *you* are the new genius on the small-business scene.

The limelight, not to mention the financial security that comes with it, might make your original objectives a distant memory, out of date with your present situation. To resist these high-profile growth possibilities is not only appealing; some would say it is downright uncharacteristic of the entrepreneur, whose very nature is to identify opportunities that most people don't see.

* * *

In Part II, I examine the common expansion traps that every growing business encounters. Whether the future problems come as the result of expanding overhead or going public, the decisions you make will ultimately determine who runs your company, how much control you keep and how much you give away, and whether your original objectives are allowed to rule.

Notes

1. Robert Townsend, *Further Up The Organization* (New York: Alfred A. Knopf, 1984), pp. 86–87.
2. Daniel H. Gray, "Uses and Misuses of Strategic Planning," *Harvard Business Review* (January–February 1986).
3. Ronaleen R. Roha, "7 Mistakes That Can Kill Your Business and How to Avoid Them," *Changing Times* (August 1988).

II

FORMS
OF
EXPANSION

Chapter 4

The Volume Trap

The small-business owner needs a dependable, consistent, and readily available factor by which to judge a company's success. Comparing gross sales from one period to the next is one of the most popular methods for evaluating business progress and success, but it has its drawbacks. For instance, there may be a vast difference between overall growth and profitable growth.

Sales volume is the standard for describing how a business succeeds over time. That's because successful companies *do* experience ever-increasing sales, often quite rapidly. Thus if you look at the history of an industry leader today you may see tremendous growth in sales volume. What's often over-looked, though, is that a successful company results from building strength in many ways beyond sales growth—expense and cost controls, customer satisfaction, the right staffing, and high-quality leadership, among them.

Rapidly increasing sales volume is not the cause of growth, nor is it the factor that defines success. Rather, it is the *result* of correctly planned and executed growth. This is the difference between sales growth, or top-line expansion, which may lead to a variety of control problems and misdirection, and planned expansion, which involves both top- and bottom-line, or profit growth. The latter is the result of operating within the guidelines of your business objective.

Choosing Your Direction

Sales volume is fairly easy to track. You know immediately at the end of each day, week, and month exactly what you've taken in. Sales are less subject to interpretation than most other indicators. And one-time adjustments in costs or expenses will not change the top line of your income statement. These are among the reasons that sales dominate the analysis of business activity. But these figures never tell the whole story, and could even tell a story that's far removed from the real truth. Remember:

> Just because an indicator is easy to track doesn't mean it's the best way to judge performance.

Example: One retail store's gross sales doubled during its second year, and then rose again by 80 percent in the third year. The owner believed this was confirmation that all was well. But during the same three years, profits remained low and there was always a shortage of cash. During the fourth year, the owner was forced to close the doors.

Sales volume, by itself does not define success, especially if the cost of that "success" is ultimately the failure of your business. Financial results can be misleading if used improperly or in isolation. For instance, tracking the wrong results will not give you the information you need to correct internal problems in time. Rather than judging your company's performance on the basis of sales growth alone, you should review the entire financial picture collectively. Sales volume may be a significant part of that analysis, but other indicators should also be included. These are indicators such as:

- Percentage of gross profit (sales minus direct costs), which shows whether you are controlling markup and points out declining margins during periods of expansion.
- Return on sales (net profit divided by sales), which more accurately reveals the real growth of your operation.

- Your own perceptions and enjoyment. What's the point of being at the head of your own company if you aren't in control of your own time?

Because the last point has nothing to do with finances, it is often rejected as a measurement of performance. From the accounting point of view, the only dependable standards involve numbers. But you know that it is the intangibles that really determine success. That's what motivated you to go into business in the first place, and that's what will ultimately determine whether your decision was justified.

To stay in control of growth, you can track a number of indicators. In the long run, you will build permanent expansion by ensuring that costs and expenses remain at reasonable levels, rather than allowing gross and net margins to deteriorate.

For example, you may see sales grow from $80,000 one year to $160,000 the next—double the previous level. But during that time gross profit (sales less the cost of goods sold) declines from 48 percent to 43 percent. And net profit (the bottom line) falls from 12 percent to 4 percent. In this instance, the *amount* of profit actually is lower than it was the year before:

	First Year	*Second Year*
Sales	$80,000	$160,000
Direct costs	41,600	91,200
Gross profit	$38,400	$ 68,800
Expenses	$28,800	$ 62,400
Net profit	$ 9,600	$ 6,400

In this example, the gross margin declined. By cutting the gross margin, the higher volume is possible. But this is profitable *only* if overhead expenses are also held in check. In this case, expenses rose from $28,800 to $62,400—and that is what erodes profits.

Gross *profit* is the net of sales, less direct costs. The gross *margin* is the percentage of gross profit, and it is computed by dividing gross profit by sales. This is an important test of expansion. As long as an acceptable gross margin is maintained, that's usually a sign that you're controlling growth. However, when the gross margin declines, that may be a sign that you are losing the expansion game, unless higher volume justifies the change. For example, you may lower prices to create higher volume, knowing you will increase profits because expenses are fixed.

Healthy sales volume occurs when gross profit is maintained and when the *amount* of expenses is stabilized. This doesn't mean that expenses won't rise, only that the rate of increase should be slower than the increase in sales for the same period.

This relationship is illustrated in Figure 4-1. Note that the sales and direct costs lines rise at the same angle, but the rate of change in expenses is less and that expenses tend to rise in plateaus rather than steadily increasing with higher volume. The plateau effect results from careful and diligent expense

Figure 4-1.   Healthy volume curve.

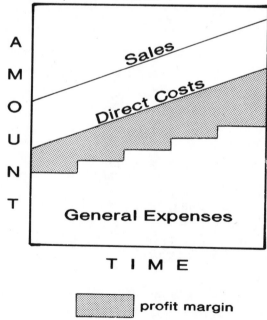

controls during expansion periods. For example, suppose you hire new employees and lease larger facilities; the result is a higher plateau of overhead. But the expenses will not rise above that plateau as long as the range of sales volume remains within the forecast level. When expenses are controlled in this manner, the net profit margin increases with growing sales volume.

In comparison, an unhealthy growth curve has very different attributes. Profit margins decline, either because direct costs are increasing along with sales or because expenses are growing at a faster rate than sales. In a completely uncontrolled expansion period, both of these problems occur at the same time. An unhealthy growth curve is also characterized by steadily increasing expense levels, rather than by the plateau effect. The unhealthy curve is illustrated in Figure 4-2.

Some aberrations might occur during expansion periods. The most common is an increase in the percentage of direct costs resulting from an *intentional* change in markup. For ex-

Figure 4-2.   Unhealthy volume curve.

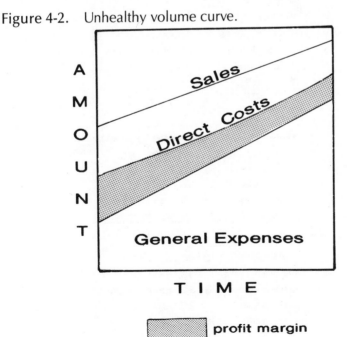

ample, suppose you lower your retail price to increase volume, which creates a lower gross margin percentage but a higher gross profit amount. As long as this tactic doesn't change overhead expenses significantly, a higher profit will result. This point is illustrated in Figure 4-3.

While this is a simplified comparison, it does illustrate the most desirable relationship when markup is changed. As gross margin shrinks, so does the relative percentage of expenses. Even though the amount of expenses increases, higher volume produces growth, in both the amount and the percentage of profit. This relationship is summarized in Figure 4-4.

You might also experience growth in overhead expenses beyond the expected plateaus during expansion, but this should be a temporary condition. It may be a normal consequence, particularly when expansion occurs rapidly, and it's acceptable as long as:

Figure 4-3.   Healthy volume comparisons.

EXAMPLE A

Sales	$ 50,000	100%
Direct Costs	30,000	60
Gross Profit	$ 20,000	40%
Expenses	15,000	30
Net Profit	$ 5,000	10%

EXAMPLE B

Sales	$ 75,000	100%
Direct Costs	48,750	65
Gross Profit	$ 26,250	35%
Expenses	18,000	24
Net Profit	$ 8,250	11%

EXAMPLE C

Sales	$100,000	100%
Direct Costs	68,000	68
Gross Profit	$ 32,000	32%
Expenses	20,000	20
Net Profit	$ 12,000	12%

Figure 4-4. Expense/profit relationship.

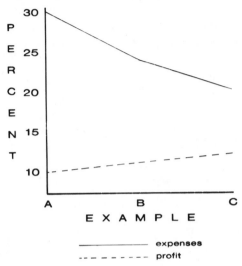

- You have anticipated the change in overhead and have budgeted for it.
- Cash flow is adequate to pay for temporarily higher overhead.
- The additional level of expense is justified by higher future sales volume and profits.
- You are able to control expenses so that they don't continue to rise above the temporarily higher level, and your results return to the normal plateau in the very near future.

Set a standard for yourself that expansion is acceptable *only* if the level of overhead increases at a slow enough rate so that profits can increase as well. You can achieve this by expressing the standard in several ways:

- Overhead levels for fixed expenses (those that should not change with sales levels) must be kept at the same level from one month to the next.
- The increase in variable expenses (those expenses that go up with increased sales volume, like travel and tele-

phone expense) must take place at a rate equal to or
lower than the percentage increase in sales.
• The overall level of expenses must not be allowed to
increase above the level of gross profit.

You can budget for expansion and develop control standards at the same time by being aware of the differences
between healthy and unhealthy change. Use a worksheet to
track each month's costs, variable and fixed expenses, and
profits. A sample worksheet is shown in Figure 4-5.

Even though variable and fixed expenses are not broken
down on this sample worksheet, you should be aware of the
distinction. Variable expense levels will change as sales increase, but not to the same degree as changes in direct costs.
Examples include salespeople's travel and transportation, telephone expenses, and advertising. Within anticipated ranges of
sales, fixed expenses will not change significantly, and you
should be able to control the plateaus of overall expenses
through diligent budgeting.

With the completed worksheet, compare monthly results
to the standards established in your forecast and budget.
Follow the actual and budgeted results each month, looking

Figure 4-5.   Tracking worksheet.

```
               Month _____


                                  AMOUNT        %
                                              ____

   sales                         _____   ____
   direct costs                  _____   ____

   gross profit                  _____   ____


   variable expenses  _____              ____
   fixed expenses                _____   ____

      total                      _____   ____

   net profit                    ═══════════   ════
```

for negative trends. First, identify what you consider a reasonable percentage for direct costs and for expenses, based on the volume you forecast for the year. Next, compare these to actual results developed on the tracking worksheet. Summarize the outcome on a tracking record like the one shown in Figure 4-6.

If the variance between budgeted and actual results begins to widen, it could mean that:

- Expansion is occurring too rapidly, and it's time to step in and slow down the rate.
- You are not controlling the level of direct costs, and will need to institute inventory controls.
- Expenses are growing at unacceptable levels, and it's time to institute direct control measures.

In some businesses, the level of variable expenses will be significant. For example, if you make direct sales, your travel, entertainment, telephone, and advertising expenses have to be budgeted realistically. However, in a service company this might not be the case. For example, when a consultant earns more money by entering contracts for more work, that should not increase direct costs or general expenses.

You can choose your own direction by establishing a realistic forecast and budget, and then staying within the boundaries you set. The real key to growth is management—not only of sales levels but also of costs and expenses. Budgets work when you set and follow the rules listed here and in Figure 4-7.

1. *Your budget must be realistic, and not just wishful thinking.* For example, if you plan to get more customers and greater sales volume this year, you will need to increase your budget for advertising. It's not realistic to forecast higher sales without also being willing to pay the cost of getting there.

2. *The budget must allow room for growth.* You can achieve expansion when you accept reasonable risks. For example, higher sales might mean hiring clerical help. Your budget will have to be increased for that expense.

Figure 4-6.   Tracking record.

MONTH	DIRECT COSTS						EXPENSES					
	BUDGET		ACTUAL		VARIANCE		BUDGET		ACTUAL		VARIANCE	
		%		%		%		%		%		%

Figure 4-7. Budgeting rules.

```
1. Your budget must be
   realistic.

2. The budget must allow
   room for growth.

3. The budget must be
   documented properly.

4. Your budget must be
   reviewed regularly.

5. You need to take
   action.
```

3. *The budget must be documented properly.* The only way you can monitor success is by making meaningful comparisons. Thus you will need to look at what actually occurs and compare it to what you planned. For example, if you arbitrarily assume that telephone expenses will go up by 1 percent per month, every month, you have no valid basis for determining whether actual expenses are reasonable. But if you control long-distance calls by using a telephone log, and you research likely rate increases, you will be able to make sound assumptions when you build your budget.

4. *Your budget must be reviewed regularly.* A monthly summary of variances, compared to the budget, will reveal problems that need correction. If you review actual and budgeted results each month, you then have a system for identifying and correcting problems before they erode profits.

5. *You need to take action.* It's not enough to merely identify where problems exist; those problems must be acted upon. For example, suppose this month's report shows that office-supply expenses are much higher than your budget allows. What does that mean? Was your budget inaccurate (meaning it should be corrected), or are you spending too much money? How can you stop the overspending so that the problem doesn't continue? What actions should you take now so that no further erosion occurs?

The budget is the real test of profitable growth. If you are able to apply the leadership and management skills necessary to keep expenses in line, while also allowing expense levels to increase so that profitable growth can occur, then you will achieve your expansion plans.

Volume and Success

Even when diligently following your budget, you face the risk of growing without the controls needed to ensure profits. Your objective should rule the rate and type of growth your business experiences.

A comparison of volume, profits, and return on sales points out a disturbing fact: Even when your sales are rising at an impressive rate, the real view of your business can be obscured. This might be the case even when you want to create a successful level of sales, and when you attempt to ensure that growth takes place in the right direction. It's easy to conclude that increasing sales must be a positive result. But you won't know how to increase profits, because the information extracted from financial results doesn't always point out what's wrong.

Let's see how this happens:

Example: Volume has been rising steadily over the past three years, but it seems there's never enough cash on hand to keep up with current bills. The problem is becoming more severe, even though sales continue to grow. Several conditions are contributing to this problem, including:

• *Increases in inventory, to the point that inventory levels are way too high.* This means too much cash is invested in inventory, even with the higher level of sales.

• *A slowdown in the time required to collect outstanding accounts receivable.* With growth in sales volume, collections are taking too long, thus cash flow is affected directly. You're not getting your money as quickly as you need it, even though sales volume is higher.

• *Higher levels of current debt, resulting from greater sales activity.* As you buy more merchandise, pay a higher level of expenses and taxes, and allow overhead to rise, you also need more cash. The stakes are higher with increased volume, so your cash flow must keep pace, otherwise growth translates to ever-growing problems in meeting your obligations.

In each of these situations, the solution is to more carefully control the use of money. Your inventory levels have to be kept at a realistic level, based on the volume of sales. Your collections must be made in a timely manner, so that the cash will be available to run your operation. And growth must be accompanied by enough working capital to pay current bills.

Financial analysis is valuable in identifying these problems and in reversing negative trends before they become crises—but only if you follow up on what you discover. If you study *only* the trend in sales, keeping score of how well you beat last year's top-line record, you might not even know there's a problem until it's too late. Your analysis must encompass all of the trends, not just sales volume.

Your judgment about the real state of your operation should go beyond growth in volume. Otherwise, you can easily be distracted from actions that should be taken today to achieve what you want. What are the reasons you started your own business? Where do you want it to go? How soon do you hope to reach your goal? In other words, what is your business objective and are the current financial trends moving you toward achieving it?

The Value of Simplicity

There are times when reducing the volume of and the risks in your business are worth more than the rewards of ever-growing volume, with the related time commitment and exposure to liability. While this may seem an obvious point, it's difficult to consciously and willingly cut back. The pressure to increase the operation's size is a real and ever-present problem, even when growth creates more problems than it solves.

For example, the owner of a public accounting firm earned an annual gross income of approximately $250,000. At that level, he was able to provide personal service to every client, meet deadlines without having to work more than forty hours a week, and hold overhead in check. He needed only three staff people, and he made a respectable profit of more than 45 percent return on sales.

Even though that was an ideal level for a one-person operation, the owner wanted to expand. His idea was that, with a larger operation, profits could be increased without losing the other positive benefits of the operation. Another firm wanted to sell its accounts, so the owner negotiated a price, took in a junior partner, and increased gross receipts to $800,000 per year. Now it was also necessary to make other changes. Staff was increased to fourteen people, the firm moved to a larger office, and money was invested in larger, more expensive accounting and tax software and a larger computer system. The hours were longer, too, especially during tax season.

Although gross receipts were much higher, the owner did not realize his goals on any level. The return on sales dropped, and so did the *amount* of profit. He was forced to increase his work week to more than sixty hours, and even more than that during tax season. The pressure was constant, and a good deal of his time was spent trying to solve problems. The owner became increasingly discontent. He missed the old days when he had time to himself, when he was in control, and when profits were greater.

His first attempt at solving the problem involved taking on even more work. The idea was that if the size of the staff was increased and another partner was added, there would be greater economy of money and time. This is the solution that many business owners turn to when their original ideas don't work out.

However, after thinking about it and studying the problem for some time, the owner decided to reduce the volume of sales rather than increase it. He sold off many of the accounts, especially those that paid too slowly and created most of the headaches. He kept only those accounts he enjoyed and that presented the fewest problems. He reduced the size of his staff, went back to a simpler computer system, and found a smaller office.

Reducing the size of the operation also allowed the owner to reduce his time at work. Profits rose, both in dollar amount and as a percentage of gross. From his experience with expanding volume, the owner discovered that every business has an ideal size, and that expanding beyond that size creates problems.

You can grow without losing quality, increasing your time commitment, or lowering your profits. But to achieve that, growth must be controlled and methodical, achieved within a carefully constructed business and marketing plan. And you need to constantly evaluate volume, and to do away with sources of income that are too costly.

You might be able to control growth so that satisfactory working conditions are possible, but that could be a different situation than a previous plateau offered. This is one of the consequences of growth, even when profits increase. Expansion can change the entire picture.

Example: An accountant who experienced problems with expansion finally realized one of the errors he'd made. He had failed to eliminate problem accounts. He had not enjoyed working with some of the people he served, either because they wanted more service than he was prepared to provide or because they were slow in paying their bills. One important lesson came from the temporary expansion: Problem volume *must* be eliminated because it costs too much money to keep it.

With an expanded income base, the owner could have better managed his operation by eliminating problem accounts before they began to dominate his time. This would also have done away with most of the collection problems. He might have been willing to give up some of the personal service and contact he'd previously enjoyed, but only if the revised environment of the operation was equally satisfying.

As the owner, you have the right to decide whom to work with, and you should exercise that right. An employee can be stuck with an unpleasant boss, with confrontive coworkers, or with tasks he or she does not enjoy. But as an owner, you are in charge, and you can decide what you will and won't do. This is more valuable than financial freedom, because it is a quality-of-life issue rather than a matter of task delegation.

Eliminating Lines of Business

In the desire to simplify, you can reduce volume that does not produce profits, or that comes with more problems than you wish to deal with. But the decision should be based on a thorough analysis, of both the nature of the work and its effect on your cash flow and profits.

Before you reduce what you consider to be unprofitable volume, be sure you understand the financial side of the transaction. You need to base the decision on a combination of factors, not just finances. But the question of real profitability might be more difficult to pin down than you think.

Example: A contractor had experienced substantial growth in volume over the past five years, and he wanted to grow even more in the future. His goal was to increase volume in the most profitable lines of business. The first plan was to eliminate activities that did not produce as much profit, freeing up the owner's time to create greater volume and higher profits by specializing in one, highly profitable line of work.

A first analysis broke down income into three major classifications: commercial building, residential building, and home renovation. A comparison of profits revealed that commercial building was the most profitable, so he decided to do away with both residential lines and spend all his time seeking more commercial work. However, when he met with his accountant, the owner realized the flaws in his original idea, and had to change the plan.

First, he'd gone into the second and third lines of business to keep crews busy during the slow season. Profits were reviewed on a year-long basis, but during the cold and wet months there was virtually no commercial work available. Second, eliminating volume would not automatically eliminate the same percentage of overhead expenses. Some of those expenses, such as the owner's salary, leases on buildings and equipment, and administrative expenses such as telephone and utilities would remain at current levels, no matter how much volume was eliminated.

A second analysis showed that simply eliminating residential lines of business would not achieve the owner's goals. In fact, although the return on sales was lower, it made more sense to do away with the commercial line, for these reasons:

1. Commercial work demanded most of the owner's time, and that would increase as commercial volume grew. Thus there was a built-in limit to the amount of growth the owner could achieve in commercial work.
2. The seasonal nature of commercial work made it impractical to do only that type of work.
3. Commercial work came with the greatest need for investment in equipment, for direct labor, and for inventory space.
4. The owner *enjoyed* home building and renovation more than commercial work.

With these points in mind, it made little sense to do away with the two lines of business that produced the lowest return on sales. A purely financial study seemed to make that the logical choice, but the broader analysis pointed the way to a less obvious decision. If nothing else, the owner's personal enjoyment dictated that commercial work be eliminated rather than residential.

In this example, the owner *wanted* to grow. But when the analysis was confined to the most profitable line of work, it was incomplete. It seemed logical at first to seek growth in the most profitable line of business—but too many other factors made this less than practical.

An analysis of all the factors in your operation may reveal that growth is best achieved by *not* doing away with seemingly unprofitable work. Pursuing the activities you enjoy the most should be a high priority. You should also be aware that less profitable work might be needed to carry you through a seasonal change or share the cost of fixed overhead. Finally, your own time demands may place a natural limit on the purely financial growth you can reasonably expect to realize.

Planning for Volume Expansion

If gross volume is your primary goal, problems related to cash flow, profits, and time commitments can be expected to follow.

Instead, the level and rate of your growth in volume must be planned, not as a primary goal but as part of a larger, coordinated expansion program. You will achieve expansion by being aware of its total nature. Sales and profits can be sustained only when your "middle lines"—costs and expenses—are kept under control, and when cash is available to feed and nurture growing volume.

It's like an army on the march. Territorial conquest might seem desirable on the map, but it's only possible when the supply lines are kept open, when the flanks are guarded, and when the vast lands conquered can be held. The success of the campaign depends entirely on the general's ability to assess risk, to plan ahead well and foresee the dangers, and to remember the big objective. Gaining too much territory too quickly can spell defeat.

Creating a volume plan is very similar to planning a military campaign: You must consider what you will need to do to support increased levels of operation. And the plan allows you to remain in control of your operation, regardless of the goals. For example, if your goal is to increase profits without a corresponding demand on your own time, that combination must dictate the rate of growth that will be possible and practical. Or if your goal is to add a new product or service line, or to serve a new geographic area, you must determine the level of sales necessary to cover costs and expenses at the break-even level or above.

It's one thing to set a goal to "increase sales by 30 percent this year" and another to prepare for and anticipate what that really means. What will you need to do now to make that growth successful? Must you increase payroll and inventory? Will you need larger facilities? What will happen to your cost and expense budget? Do you need outside financing to *afford* the growth? If your planning is thorough enough, maybe you can achieve a 40 percent increase in volume and profits. Or you might find that you'd be better off shooting for a 15 percent increase each year for the next two years instead.

In planning for growth, always coordinate expense and cash flow controls, and plan profits as well as sales. You will do well to define *success* by looking well beyond sales volume alone. Make your criteria a combination of profits, return on sales, and time commitment. Judge trends by reviewing the cost and gross profit rate, monitoring the level and change in permanent overhead, and ensuring that the direction of volume points to where you want to take the business.

The time factor is the most commonly overlooked aspect of an expansion plan. You must be realistic. For example, if you operate a service business, that means your volume and profits are limited to the maximum number of hours you have available. Expansion means you must either increase your time commitment or expand your staff. And in either case the result is limitation. Either you limit the growth or you accept higher costs and expenses to manage higher levels of sales volume.

Planned growth requires your control—a hands-on plan for achieving a clearly stated objective. The control factor comes down to determining the level and rate of growth, on your own terms. Don't passively allow volume to happen if it's contrary to what you want, or if the result is a lower return on sales. You are in control when you determine how rapidly your business will grow.

Some small-business owners fall into the trap of thinking that expansion, once it begins, is an irreversible trend. If you find yourself growing away from your objective, then evaluate the cost, expense, and cash flow realities; and take control again. Plan your growth methodically, according to the objective you have set.

* * *

Even when you recognize the trap of judging performance on the basis of volume alone, your task is not limited to a change in your own perception. If you have employees, you must also educate them in establishing priorities and judging true success. Defining your relationship with employees, and the problems you will encounter with staff, is the topic of the next chapter.

Chapter 5
The People Trap

Expanding the volume of a business often means an accompanying growth in staff. For many types of businesses, the support staff is a predictable part of the expansion process—a reality that can't be ignored. There are two ways to expand staff: (1) in response to a perceived need for more help as an inevitable consequence of success and (2) as part of a carefully planned, timed, and coordinated management decision.

This chapter examines the question of employee expansion on two levels. First is expanding the number of employees, and the changes that makes in the tone of your operation. Second is the quality of life in your company, the tendency to add management layers, allow paperwork to increase, and fall victim to bureaucracy.

By carefully controlling the timing and rate of growth in your employee base, you can achieve your goals through an expanded employee base and, at the same time, maintain the efficiency and effectiveness of response to your customer.

As you add more staff, you'll find the business environment changes as well. Overhead grows, not only because more people are on the payroll, but for related expenses: higher rent for larger facilities, payroll taxes, insurance and other benefits, and a higher level of office supplies, telephones, and other expenses.

The policies you establish that plan for and allow staff

growth should define and match future requirements. For example, when you know the level of geographic and sales expansion planned for the next two to three years, you can also plan a corresponding increase in marketing and support staff. The growth policies you establish are expressed in terms of budgets, personnel policies, competitive benefits, and facilities.

The planning involved in expanding staff goes back to your stated objective. The business objective defines growth and its limitations. The timing, capital requirements, and quality of business life all rest on adding staff both to manage new levels of work and also to avoid surprises. Imagine how disruptive it is to suddenly have to hire people because your staff is swamped in paperwork—when there's no desk space, no budget, and no plan. If your business objective rules the timing of staff expansion, a budget will exist. And if you know many months in advance that you will be adding more people, then you will also be prepared for expansion of facilities, middle management levels, and internal procedures.

Beyond the financial changes and the higher stakes involved with an expanding staff, you may find another change occurring. When you increase the number of employees, you must ensure that the working environment remains both efficient and controlled. To do this, you need to delegate many tasks by creating a middle-management level. But you can't delegate control over the tone and philosophy in your organization's culture. You need to avoid creating a bureaucracy or allowing others to set a tone contrary to your interests as owner.

While having a large number of employees on hand might be necessary, there can be alternatives. This does not mean that a business should avoid hiring. It does mean that (1) during periods of staff expansion you must be aware of the need for strong and direct management; and (2) there might be sensible alternatives to creating an ever-expanding staff.

The Departmental Mentality

In a very small company it is fairly simple to create a sense of teamwork. Everyone works toward the same goals, because the president is there every day and the goals are expressed directly. But as the company grows and separate departments are created, goals and motives change: The interests of the organization may become secondary to the interests and priorities of one manager; conflict may develop between managers and between departments; egos become involved, and individuals may become aware of the relative levels of power within the company. The desirable single purpose of the small business can be lost in the process. You can avoid this by watching for the signs and defusing the problem before it becomes so large there's nothing you can do about it.

Example: A distribution company had fourteen branch offices and three home office employees. At that level, the president was able to have direct contact with the entire staff on a daily basis. But as the regional influence of the firm grew, and as the number of branch offices increased, it became necessary to expand the home office staff. By the end of the fifth year, there were twenty-four employees in the home office, divided into five distinct departments. Daily contact with top management was limited. At the end of the seventh year, the company's headquarters had moved to a larger facility and sixty-five employees were divided into eleven departments. The owner had delegated virtually the entire home-office management function. Unfortunately, morale and efficiency were at an all-time low. Political conflict, bureaucracy, and self-interest had invaded what was once a small, efficient team. Also, profits were down. When he compared the present to the past, the owner was mystified that the business was now earning less.

In this case, the problem is inescapably one of lack of management at the top. These negative changes can't be blamed on leadership in the middle ranks, nor on the lack of loyalty at staff levels. If top management ignores the situation, a decline in quality and morale is inevitable. But you can achieve growth of volume and territory—even when accompanied by rapid expansion of staff—with the proper involvement and control. You can maintain efficiency and avoid bureaucracy and self-interest.

Example: The founder of a real estate brokerage firm recruited a number of sales agents over the course of four years. Eventually several branch offices were opened, so that the firm penetrated a two-county market. During the expansion period, administrative staff grew from one person to more than twenty. This included accounting, bookkeeping, legal, clerical, and marketing staff members. However, on an administrative level, the company continued to operate as efficiently as when it had only one office.

Here the owner remained directly involved on a daily basis. He held weekly staff meetings, with the entire administrative staff involved. A key employee functioned as office manager, but stayed in close contact with the owner. Every employee was part of the management process. There was no layer of isolation between the top and the bottom. The problems associated with growth were aired openly and resolved as a team effort. Problems were avoided because the owner—who ultimately is responsible for the success or failure of staff expansion—recognized the need to remain in touch.

Confronting the Problems of Growth

When quality and efficiency fall, expenses rise. The relationship is direct and inevitable. A retrospective look at the problem shows that a decline in corporate quality of life is likely to occur when the owner steps away from day-to-day operations.

This does not mean that you can never escape the mundane routines. On the contrary, effective leaders must be able to delegate, to create a middle layer and depend on others to monitor conditions. But oversight must continue. Don't confuse appropriate delegation with removal from primary responsibility; ensure that the actions of your staff are meeting your objectives.

Remember that employees view your job differently from how you see it. Employees see management's job as one of guidance and direction. You are responsible for ensuring that their work environment is guided by correctly motivated middle managers. The direction you take enables them to work under fairly secure, satisfying conditions.

Look for signs of problems related to staffing and communication, as shown in Figure 5-1 and then take the action steps described in the following sections to reverse the negative trends that develop.

Growth in Paper Work

It's accurate to say that when your middle managers ask permission to buy more file space, it's time to step in and take a close look at changes in your operation. Look for signs of increasing paper work; the development of forms, increased printing expenses, and unnecessary interdepartmental paper flow are signs that a bureaucracy is growing. If you don't minimize this trend, it can choke your operation, lead to expensive staff expansion just to handle the internal work, and result in a decline in profits. It's human nature to forget about the customer and to begin structuring departments to serve perceived internal needs rather than outside markets. You must ensure that every procedure, form, memo, and report ultimately serves your business objective.

Figure 5-1.   Signs of staffing problems.

1. **Growth in paper work.**

2. **Self–interest in middle management requests.**

3. **Conflicts between departments.**

4. **Rapid staff expansion.**

5. **Expanding middle management layers.**

6. **Expanding executive layers.**

7. **Increasing frequency of meetings.**

8. **Rapid turnover.**

Action steps: When you recognize that a complicated paper work system is growing in your company, call a meeting of the managers or staff people who are involved in procedurial decisions. Review the paper work now being used, as well as proposed new forms and reports. Pay special attention to paper flow between departments. Question everything. State your goal to reduce rather than increase the amount of paperwork. Ask each person in the meeting to devise a method to achieve this, and set a deadline for the response.

Example: An office-equipment company increased its inventory when public response was greater than anticipated. Accompanying a period of volume expansion, the owner added clerical staff, bought a computer, and developed systems to track back orders, customer requests or complaints, and market response. Within one year, a number of internal forms and reports had developed, but the problems associated with growth were as severe as before. A review of paperwork showed that problems were not being solved, only being kept in more organized files. A complete internal revision simplified the process and, at the same time, freed up staff time to solve problems rather than to fill out forms.

Self-Interest in Middle Management Requests

In a small company, the tendency among employees is to discuss what "we" need to do to solve problems or reach goals. But as the company becomes departmentalized, those same issues are often discussed in terms of what "I" want for "my department." Whether this means a manager is pursuing self-interest above the interests of the company, or is creating a departmental priority attitude, it's time to get the team back together.

Action steps: Accept responsibility for setting the tone in the organization. As your company grows, this becomes a critical role for the owner. Begin holding weekly meetings including all department managers (or, if staff level is under twenty people, with *all* employees). State your goals as clearly and as specifically as possible: The company must work to-gether toward a singular goal; individual or departmental interests will not be given priority. Keeping your hand in during staff expansion is the best way to prevent a departmental or self-interest attitude taking over.

Example: The president of a software manufacturing firm spent a good deal of time on the road. It seemed that whenever he returned to the office, a number of managers and executives wanted to meet privately to discuss an important issue. In increasing numbers, the requests were oriented toward a department's needs. It seemed that managers had lost sight of what the owner wanted for the company. He concluded it was time to cut back on travel and to begin holding weekly staff meetings, so as to emphasize *company* priorities and reestablish a team approach.

Conflicts Between Departments

You will learn a great deal about how the business's tone is changing just by listening to what your employees tell you. When you begin to hear about internal, departmental conflicts, that's a danger sign. A problem is emerging, and it must be solved immediately.

Action steps: As soon as one manager or employee communicates a problem that involves someone else in the company, immediately get the two people together. Listen to both sides of the issue, and then emphasize that the company's goals must be met, not the goals of individuals or departments. Propose a solution to the conflict, or give the individuals the option of working it out on their own. Identify the causes of the problem, and correct the situation so it is resolved once and for all.

At first glance, personal conflicts seem especially difficult to resolve because you don't always know the source; the problem is not easily defined. In addition, opposing groups tend to think in absolutes: "Someone else is causing the problem, someone else is completely wrong, someone else is refusing to work with me." When both sides of an issue are examined, though, you will be able to define the problem and find a reasonable solution.

Rapid Staff Expansion

Once you see the support staff growing at a rate greater than you anticipated, stop and take a close look. Chances are, managers are adding staff members at a greater rate than needed.

Action steps: Remember that as long as you don't control staff expansion, it will occur on its own—often at an excessive and unnecessary pace. Never let go completely of your direct involvement in approving staff additions. Question the proposal to hire more people and look for alternatives. Approve more hiring only when there is no way to solve work-related problems at current staff levels. If you allow managers to expand their staffs without critical review, the payroll will expand unnecessarily.

Example: The president of a marketing company was concerned about recent staff increases. During the past six months, the staff had grown from thirteen employees to over thirty. Profits were down, mainly because of much higher overhead. The problem came to the president's attention when the vice-president suggested the company be relocated to a larger facility. Instead, the president called together all the managers and gave them a collective priority: there must be no more staff increases without the president's review and approval.

Expanding Middle Management Layers

How many new departments were created during the last six months? Were they all necessary? If your company is growing so rapidly that you must also add new departments, ensure that net profits are also keeping pace.

Action steps: As you find your internal staff being divided into expanding departments, review the structure of the company. Remember that departments, by their nature, are separate. The more separation you have, the more difficult it is to create a singular team. Consider revising that structure, and review all proposed departmental expansions with the purpose of reducing the creation of new sections.

Example: When an owner created her small import business, the idea had been to keep things simple. But during the past year, four new departments had been created. When the accountant suggested creating three separate departments under his own control, the owner drew the line. There would be no more internal expansion without a complete preview of a specific problem, and no decision would be made until every alternative had been explored. She made it clear that solutions would be developed without creating a massive superstructure within the company.

Expanding Executive Layers

Morale declines most rapidly when a company becomes top-heavy. Many small companies expand to the point where thirty to forty people are on staff, with as many as one-third that total consisting of vice-presidents and other executives. This is the least efficient situation of all.

Action steps: Keep an eye on the payroll ratio between executives and other groups. When the percentage of executive salaries creeps upward, take action. Also watch the numbers. Don't fall into the trap of thinking that emerging problems will be solved by hiring another executive. The real work is done by the rank and file. Bringing in more chiefs only leads to greater problems and higher expenses in the future.

Example: The owner of a fifteen-store retail chain attended an executive staff meeting. Rapid volume growth led to several administrative problems, and solutions were proposed and discussed. One attendee suggested that additional executives be hired to solve the problems. The owner responded by saying that no new executives were needed, and that the current leadership would have to work with the resources already on the payroll.

Increasing Frequency of Meetings

Keep an eye on the number of meetings being held in your company. A meeting should be an effective forum for departments to communicate and solve common problems. But action takes place after the meeting, not during it. As the number and frequency of meetings grow, action declines.

Action steps: Keep an eye on how many meetings are held in your company. You might conduct one weekly meeting with the key managers and executives involved and, in some instances, other meetings will be necessary. But don't let the opportunity to meet and determine action become a problem. If your leadership team spends all its time in meetings, no one is on the front line, in the action. As owner, you have the power to put an end to unnecessary meetings.

Example: The president of an engineering firm was frustrated because project managers were spending an increasing proportion of their time in meetings. His attempts at reducing meeting time were not producing results, however, so he instituted a new procedure. The leader of each meeting would now be responsible for writing a report and submitting it to the president within one day after the meeting. That report would answer several questions: what was on the agenda? what decisions were made? and what actions will now be taken to solve the problem? As a result of the new report, the number of meetings declined by one-half within a month.

Rapid Turnover

Perhaps the most dependable indicator of staff expansion problems is an increase in employee turnover. This often is a symptom that the staff is being expanded incorrectly. If you notice that employees leave the company and must be replaced during their first year, and if that trend seems to be on the rise, look carefully at the quality of leadership in the middle. You may find a need for more direct involvement as your staff expands.

Action steps: Your task is to look for signs of self-interest above company interest. If a manager has been given a supervisory role but fails to pursue the company's interests, you can expect worthwhile employees to go elsewhere. Take a direct role, review staffing trends, and make whatever changes are necessary in middle management. This might demand some tough decisions, but remember that as long as you delegate responsibility and authority to others, you have a duty to every employee. You must ensure that their jobs have validity, and that they are being led appropriately. When that's not the case, the overall quality of your staff will decline through attrition. Remain directly involved and correct emerging turnover problems before they take over.

Example: In reviewing the past year, the president of a small company was concerned about the turnover level. Among a total staff of about twenty employees, eight people were replaced during the twelve months. Many of these were concentrated in two departments. He called each manager into his office, expressed his concern, and asked them to explain why turnover was so high. He also gave each manager a new goal: Reduce turnover by solving the problems that create it.

The Power and Influence Problem

As your organization grows in terms of territory, volume, and people, you will need to delegate authority. And when that occurs, you confront the element of human nature that inevitably finds its way into a business culture. In a growing company, middle management becomes aware of the power and influence of the decision-making process.

The equation is a simple one in theory, but it presents a complicated challenge in practice. The more there is at stake, the more important power and influence become. If certain managers have the power to make decisions, or to influence you in the decisions you make, they have more control over their lives and the lives of the staff—or at least that's the theory.

In practice, awareness of power and influence are unspoken factors, yet the desire to increase them are seen in many ways. Some managers equate their relative influence in terms of the number of employees in their department. Thus the more people who report to them, the greater their influence. Other managers view their influence in terms of the strategic location of the department, the size of their office, or the number of meetings they attend.

Even the best-motivated individual might end up playing the power and influence game. It's a problem in companies of all sizes—and even shows up in any situation where people get together, including fraternal organizations, scouting, and the local PTA. As energy-wasting and pointless as it might seem, the problems caused by political motives cannot be ignored. They have a direct impact on profitability and product or service quality.

You can't completely do away with political motives, nor can you ignore the problem. But as the leader of your company, you can show by your actions that self-interests do not lead to results and are not tolerated. Confront the issues directly. Raise problems in front of a group of managers, and don't allow individuals to corner you in one-on-one meetings, especially for decisions that affect other people and departments. Reject requests made in the hallway or over lunch. Respect your middle management team enough to insist that everyone be involved in a final decision, and everyone hears the request before a decision is made.

A hindsight look at staff expansion often reveals the growth of a problem. A small, effective company grows rapidly and staff increases follow. As that occurs, top management loses touch with the people who do the work, and quality falls as a result. Profits erode, and eventually the owner is faced with a larger problem: either close the doors or take drastic action to eliminate the problem.

A common misconception is that staff must increase with growth and so must bureaucracy. But in fact that is not the case; a successful operation does always need to add staff. However, efficiency should improve with staff growth. This is essential to the continued success of your operation. The most successful companies are built on a foundation of internal communication, not on bureaucracy.

Solving Staffing Problems

Your level of contact and direct involvement often spells the difference between profitable staff growth and ever-increasing problems. It could be that your actions—out on the road—create problems for your staff and management rather than further your own objective. In the frustration of trying to keep up with an energetic, entrepreneurial owner, your key employees might see additional staff as the only solution to the rapidly changing environment you create. This occurs either as response to volumes of new business currently coming in or in anticipation of changes likely to occur in coming months. In either case, you should not ignore the problems that arise in your absense.

A second problem comes up when, owing to lack of attention on an owner's part, a manager or executive takes steps to build departmental or divisional power and influence. You will recognize this emerging problem if you look for it; take quick action to reverse the situation.

Example: An owner realized that his marketing director was creating a power base through departmental alliances and other polarizing actions. He hesitated to act at first because the individual had been successful in creating new markets. However, as time went by, the negative influence of the marketing director on other departments became impossible to ignore. The owner met with the director and explained his point of view. He sent the message that the situation must change, or the director would be replaced.

That's a tough message, but it must be delivered in no uncertain terms. If you tolerate a progressively deteriorating situation, hoping it will stabilize or disappear on its own, then you're heading in the wrong direction and allowing the problem to escalate. A well-motivated individual will appreciate your candor and take steps to reverse the trend.

You can't expect an intimate, friendly atmosphere to remain in effect when you expand a small staff to a moderate or large one. Expansion requires a different environment, but it can remain healthy. You can ask for and get positive responses when you spot negatives and instruct key people to reverse them. Tolerating the problem is not the answer. Neither is accepting it as inevitable, since that admits you can't manage a growing business. These are contrary to the positive attributes a business owner must have, and to the actions you want to exercise.

If you attempt to correct the problems of staff expansion and do not succeed, consider another course—bringing a halt to further growth. This might prove necessary, as either a temporary or a permanent measure.

Example: The owner of a public relations firm had always reviewed all work before it was sent to clients. But during a period of expansion, he delegated this task to account managers. Opposing camps developed within the company, staff morale fell, and the quality of work suffered. When the owner finally realized what had occurred, he asked each account manager for his or her ideas and positive, constructive solutions. None had any answers that were useful.

After thinking about the problem for a few days, the owner decided to take action. He called together the entire staff and described the problem as he perceived it. He then announced that no new clients would be accepted, no promotions or salary increases would be granted, no new employees would be added, and the current operating budget would be reviewed weekly and strictly enforced. These measures were to remain in effect indefinitely. In addition, the president insisted on review of all work before it went to clients, without exception. "From this day forward," the owner stated, "I'm the account manager on every account."

The owner's direct involvement did at least halt the development of the problems. At the same time, he accepted responsibility for the environment within his company. The situation had come about because he'd let go of the direct involvement he'd once practiced. The new control measures were not lifted until the owner was convinced that a more positive internal situation had been created— and that took many months and great effort. In the end, though, the owner wrestled control back from the system. At that point, a more gradual, methodical rate of volume expansion was allowed to occur, with a greater portion of the owner's time devoted to internal, hands-on involvement.

Creating Alternative Career Paths

When you hire someone to work for you, that action brings with it a responsibility to the individual. It extends beyond paying a salary and providing a desk and chair. You know from your own experience that providing the contractual essentials is not enough to keep valuable people on the job.

You will be a successful owner by leading in ways beyond the payment of money. You need to allow your employees to find and pursue career paths, to expand within the organization in ways that help the individual as well as the company. People desire growth, but when positive forms of growth are not provided, they often create their own power and influence bases. Thus internal conflict and defensiveness are built up, and your business goals take second place or are lost altogether.

The most effective way to avoid these all too common problems and to create a positive, cooperative team is to allow employees to achieve a sense of satisfaction, to develop a lasting career goal, and to experience a sincere involvement in the work of your company. The traditional method of employee growth is to gradually receive promotions and raises, to accumulate vesting levels in a retirement plan, and to gain the experience that comes from succeeding on the job. However, these benefits should be the result of working in the positive environment you create, not be the end in itself.

You can take several steps to help employees build their careers while working for you, as shown in Figure 5-2 and discussed as follows.

1. *Promote existing employees before expanding your staff.* To maintain morale, demonstrate your loyalty to your current staff by promoting from within whenever possible. Even if giving an employee a promotion means you will have to spend money to train the individual, show that you're willing to take that step before bringing in a new manager or supervisor.

2. *Ask employees to set career goals, and to communicate those goals to you.* Many people never set conscious goals for themselves. Thus they do not experience the satisfaction of reaching a difficult and challenging goal as part of their professional lives. You will help your staff to improve themselves by sharing with them what you have learned about planning. The positive attributes you put to work as a business owner can just as effectively be transferred and applied to employees.

Figure 5-2. Steps to helping employees.

1. **Promote existing employees.**

2. **Ask employees to set career goals.**

3. **Allow employees to define their own jobs.**

4. **Consider giving up part of your equity.**

5. **Reward exceptional work.**

3. *Allow employees to define their own jobs within the limitations of your requirements.* Few actions will motivate employees more than allowing them to define a department or individual job. Your staff is in the best position to know what improvements should be made to existing procedures and systems. And when they're able to match those needs to their own interests, and especially when you're flexible enough to give them that freedom, motivation and morale improve. Employee loyalty becomes a tangible and lasting reality.

4. *Consider giving up part of your equity.* When an employee becomes so valuable to you that you can't afford to lose him or her, consider giving up some of your equity. If you own 100 percent of your company, allowing someone else to assume a minority ownership position will give the person a different and beneficial point of view. Instead of just working for you, he or she becomes aware of profits and long-term considerations that only an owner can appreciate. And your action will keep that employee interested in the job, rather than leaving to work for someone else.

5. *Reward exceptional work.* Recognition is important to people; in some cases it's more important than position or salary. A raise is quickly forgotten, but praise and recognition create a positive, healthy environment.

The reward should not consist of certificates, plaques, and other appearances of recognition. Those ploys are transparent to everyone, and your staff quickly tires of a public relations effort in place of real reward. Besides acknowledging an accomplishment, you should be willing to share unexpected profits by way of bonus plans, to promote deserving employees, and to make exceptionally hard-working employees part-owners of your profitable, growing organization.

Ideas for Personal Expansion

From the employee's point of view, working for a company is much more than a necessity. Most of a person's waking hours are spent at work, so a job represents a major commitment and part of life. People have interests in their own future and concerns beyond the product or service your company sells.

You can help employees to grow by offering programs that go beyond satisfying an employment commitment. These programs reduce turnover, build loyalty, and mark your company as an exceptional place to work. And the expense of providing these programs is paid back in improved morale, effort, and attitude.

Consider the following ideas to encourage personal expansion for your employees:

1. *Create internal training programs.* Offer employees free training on company time, in subject areas that will help advance their careers. The employer-provided training program should emphasize areas in which you can use the skills learned. Some employees might end up leaving and using those skills for the benefit of other employers. But by providing free training, you give them the opportunity to learn, not only at your expense, but for your benefit as well. This can only help your organization, by creating skills you will find valuable after expansion.

2. *Reimburse educational expenses.* As an employee benefit, offer to reimburse employee educational expenses. You will

want to establish limits and rules. For example, you should include these provisions as part of your policy:

    a. You will reimburse up to a specified annual maximum dollar amount.
    b. Reimbursement will be made only after the employee receives a passing grade.
    c. Only courses in business subjects will be approved as part of the program.

    3. *Send employees to educational seminars.* When seminars and other training programs are offered to corporate employees, send your people. You will want to pre-approve these activities in order to control educational expense levels. However, getting ideas from other professionals can lead to many improvements in your company, so this is a worthwhile investment.

    4. *Create incentives for education.* Offer work-related incentives to employees who improve themselves through education. These incentives might include salary increases, promotions, or both. Thus, not only do you pay the cost of education, but you also reward the employee who improves his or her professional value to you.

    5. *Offer programs beyond those that are strictly work related.* Companies that recognize their responsibility to employees are also aware that personal needs or problems often require help beyond what the employment contract demands. Be willing to offer company-paid help, including child care and professional counseling for money management or financial planning, family problems, or gambling and substance abuse.

    Some owners of small companies assume that these programs are too expensive, and that only the largest and most profitable organizations can afford them. However, if you want to expand in terms of your employees' quality of life, recognize that their lives include matters beyond the job. When viewed as ways to reduce the cost of turnover, build loyalty, and create an organization that lets individuals expand with you, the cost of these programs is not excessive.

Future Trends

One of the challenges you face as your business grows is reconciling the conflicting work environments of different size companies. In a small company, the close contact of a limited staff allows effectiveness and teamwork, but profits are limited. In a large company, the opportunity for higher profits exists, but may come at the expense of internal morale and conditions.

How can expansion be achieved without losing a friendly and close corporate culture? If expansion is gradual and controlled, a degree of small-business atmosphere can be maintained, but it will eventually give way to progress and greater efficiency. A key element in making expansion work is your own direct involvement, and not only in financial review. Involvement also means attending meetings and staying in touch with the decision-making process, being aware of staff attitudes and morale, and catching and reversing negative trends before they become large and unmanageable.

Companies and cultures mature, as do individuals. It's possible that in the future, expanding organizations—even those that depend on people to develop sales—will not need an ever-growing staff. The use of outside firms for labor-intensive functions might increase, through automated processing services or employee-leasing companies. This will happen if facility costs rise owing to limited space, and when the cost of maintaining employees is greater than the cost of hiring outside or independent help.

Home-based workers today supply labor to companies, with contact often limited to an automated network. With increasing efficiency and low cost in computers, this trend might grow in the future. At the same time, the market for middle-level expertise may decline as top management turns increasingly to its existing staff for solutions to its problems. This will affect your small business if you expect to require support services in an expanding future operation.

These ideas are well summarized by the Kiplinger Washington editors:

> The years ahead will see a continuing shift from
> top-down to lateral authority and communication

in many companies. Top management won't surrender its authority, but will share more of it. Growth in employee-consultation systems is certain. More and more firms will draw on the expertise of people on the production floor or in the delivery mainstream. Less attention will be paid to young corporate-finance wizards with their MBA degrees; too many corporations have gotten burned in recent years by following the advice of green "strategic planners" far removed from the reality of daily operations.[1]

If the trend of the future is toward *not* expanding the size of a staff but, rather, toward a more participative form of management, then many opportunities will arise for you as a business owner. If the political factors resulting from expansion can largely be removed, your task is simplified. However, it would be a mistake to suggest that self-interest or negative postures will ever be completely erased. You will still need to keep an eye on trends as they emerge. Maintenance and leadership can never be fully delegated or, once assigned to someone else, ignored.

* * *

Staff expansion is often necessary because you want to grow geographically. You may find that even starting up a second location creates tremendous problems, not just in staffing, but in maintaining profit expectations as well. This is the topic of the next chapter.

Notes

1. Kiplinger Washington Editors, *The New American Boom*, (Washington, D.C.: Kiplinger, 1987), p. 212.

Chapter 6
The Geography Trap

Whether your business sells products or services, initial success might inspire you to seek geographic expansion. A limited territory provides only a finite market. Competition, capital resources, and population all limit what you can achieve locally. However, as many small business owners have discovered, adding territory and outlets complicates the entire management function.

It's not accurate to say that two outlets are twice as difficult to manage as one. But the complications are much greater whenever you operate from more than a single location. Supervising staff, controlling expenses and cash flow, and ensuring the quality of what you sell all place demands on your time and effort. Geographic expansion can be accomplished successfully, but the process increases your risks.

The Desire to Expand

If geographic expansion were an easy move, a greater number of small businesses would have multiple outlets. Many businesses who have tried to open a second store or office have not been able to duplicate the success they experienced in one outlet; often they abandon their expansion idea after the first year.

Example: Two partners who owned a small restaurant had experienced two years of success. They decided to open a second restaurant in the next town and duplicate that success, on the premise that they now understood the formula for making the enterprise work. After four months they concluded that it was a mistake, and decided to close after the first year, when the second lease ran out.

A number of things went wrong. Running the first restaurant already took both partners' time. The effort needed to supervise employees, order food, cook and clean, and control cash proved to be full time. The second location was too great a burden, and many of the most demanding tasks could not be delegated—the entire operation was too new to assign tasks to others. The second outlet was not as profitable as the first, and recapturing the investment in equipment and furnishings would take much longer than either partner had anticipated. And the energy they had to invest in trying to make it work simply wasn't worth the effort.

The desire to expand is natural for an entrepreneur. In fact, the drive to expand may be part of the excitement and freedom that characterize the entrepreneurial experience. But the problems brought on by geographic expansion often don't justify the effort. Still, many very successful operations have started out small and have grown to national chains through franchising or direct operation. How is this achieved?

Several elements must be present in order for geographic expansion to work, beyond the obvious need for capital and market demand. These include:

1. *Delegation of on-site responsibilities.* A one-owner operation demands on-site management on a full-time basis, at least for the first one to three years. Only when the initial start-up hurdles are overcome can the owner delegate management routines to someone else.

Attempting to expand too soon creates a vacuum in on-site management. Even a two-person partnership often is developed because each partner brings a particular skill to the operation; so splitting the efforts of two people can still lead to problems. To open a second location, you need to develop an internal system that works well enough to hand it over to a trusted manager—and building that system takes time.

Example: Two partners in a retail computer store decided to open an additional store. One was a skilled marketing expert, the other an excellent supervisor and administrator. They realized that a second location would create a strain on their time and effort, so before proceeding they recruited and hired an additional manager. They put the manager in charge of running the first store. Only then did they proceed with their expansion plans.

2. *Continued oversight of operations.* The rate of geographic expansion has a natural limit. You can create efficient layers of management and control, but that takes careful planning, effort, and time. Expansion cannot occur rapidly without a well-controlled reporting chain.

Example: Two independent secretarial service owners combined their businesses into a single partnership with two offices. When they decided to open a third location, they discovered it was not enough simply to hire a manager and provide instructions and operating guidelines. Even after the reins of on-site management were handed over to the new manager, the owners had to continue monitoring the operation. They discovered that it was not possible to just hand over the task of running a shop to someone else and walk away from it. An employee, they realized, could not be expected to run the operation with the same care or concern as an owner. The fact is that only someone who has risked his or her own capital can possibly take care of a business as diligently as you do yourself.

3. *Support staff.* You might be puzzled to find that a second outlet doesn't run as smoothly as the first. What you might overlook is the difference it makes when you aren't there every day. You might recruit the same caliber of people for a second store as you hired in the first, but they will not respond to your management in the same way unless you are visible and present every day. After some time, you will be able to delegate daily management routines. But because you can't be in two places at once, this is often the most difficult element in geographic expansion.

Example: The owner of a small art gallery opened a second store and put a manager in charge. But she was busy running the first store and wasn't able to be on site every day. It took more than a year to produce the expected level of profits in the second location, but that meant the owner had to spend as much time as possible in the second location, working with the manager to ensure the gallery was run as profitably as possible.

What's the secret? How do multiple-outlet stores and service companies expand from one location to two, three, five, ten, or a hundred? Many well-run companies are, indeed, operated over a wide territory.

The secret is that a well-capitalized organization must be expanded methodically and with a good deal of work. The emphasis must be on recruiting top-caliber executive management to operate remote locations; they must operate with the owner's oversight; and the work must be accompanied by excellent control and reporting systems. This is not the same as bureaucracy. In fact, a paper-heavy operation attempting to operate in a remote area will have great difficulty operating efficiently and profitably.

Example: The owner of a retail men's and boy's clothing operation opened his first store in November. During the first two months, net profits were more than $80,000, so the owner's first thought was to expand to another store. He hesitated, though, because he knew that the one operation already demanded all his time. He was already putting in more than seventy hours a week. As things turned out, the rate of profit could not be repeated every month, because the last two months of the year were the highest volume period. Profits between January and July averaged about $6,000 per month; the big-volume times were August through September (back to school) and November and December (holiday buying period).

The owner went through the first eighteen months without opening a second store. Then he decided the time was right. He had found a store manager and delegated the time-consuming daily tasks—merchandise ordering and stocking, employee supervision, balancing cash, paying bills, and handling the phone. This freed up the owner's time, but he did not walk away from the day-to-day operation. He still insisted on signing every check and reviewing payments carefully, on checking the reconciliation of each day's bank deposit, and on inventory and purchasing controls.

Only when the first store was operating efficiently did the owner consider expanding to a second location. A big factor in this decision was his own time commitment. Now that the first operation was running smoothly, he was able to execute his control duties in two to three hours per day. This allowed him the time to research a location and take steps to open a second store.

By following the same formula that had worked so well for him before, the owner succeeded with the second store. But the first six months demanded the majority of his time. He spent most of the day at the second store, as a hands-on manager. Only when he found a second capable manager was he able to reduce his own commitment.

In this example, the owner applied two skills. Not only did he have a sense of merchandising but he was also a capable leader. He was able to recruit and train managers who could be trusted to run stores with a degree of diligence that would allow him to be elsewhere—without losing the quality and control needed in a business that ran a high volume of cash.

Within six years, the owner had formed a corporation. The original store manager became a 40 percent owner, and together they now ran thirteen stores. A national chain made an offer to buy them out, and they retired from the business with a considerable profit.

The Expansion Risk

From an outsider's point of view, the formula for geographic expansion might look simple. If the first store is a success, you open another, and then another. In theory, the profits are duplicated in each location and there's no limit to how far it can go. But anyone who has experienced running multiple outlets knows that there's a great deal more involved.

Geographic expansion—like all types of growth—increases your risks in every respect. Creating profits when you're there every day is a challenge in itself. Duplicating the experience as a remote owner is much more difficult.

These realities must be remembered when geographic expansion is considered:

1. *If you are having cash-flow problems in one location, the problem will be multiplied by opening another location.* Some small

business owners have tried to open a second outlet to solve cash-flow problems. The theory is, "I won't have to duplicate all of my overhead with two stores, so I'll be able to generate a higher return." The reality is that a second outlet only makes cash-flow problems worse. You can't afford the risk of geographic expansion until you have cash flow firmly under control.

Example: The owner of a retail kitchen goods store suffered cash-flow problems during spring and summer months, and she opened a second store in an attempt to solve the problem. Unfortunately, volume was just as poor in the second store, and the cash-flow problem became worse than before.

Example: The owner of a local bookstore discovered that volume was heaviest in fall and winter months. She ran her operation for two years and concluded that the fall and winter volume carried her through the rest of the year. She timed the opening of her second store in early fall, but only after eliminating cash-flow problems the first store had during its start-up phase. By timing the decision and then continuing to monitor the managers in both stores, the expansion succeeded.

2. *Capital must be available to carry a second location for at least six months.* Even the most cautious planner might forget what's involved in a start-up. One mistake that has been repeated by many entrepreneurs is to assume that an existing and thriving business has adequate resources to carry a second outlet. Never assume this without thorough research and analysis. Remember that capital must be committed to cover operating losses, to build inventory, and to invest in fixed assets.

The commitment of capital and coverage of operating losses is easily overlooked by an enthusiastic owner. But the risk is not only that the second outlet could fail but that it could also bring down the existing, successful store.

Example: When the owner of a bakery decided to open a second store, he thought he had good reasons to expect success. The first location was operating at capacity and producing profits every month. What he overlooked in the decision was the investment he would have to make in expensive baking equipment, shelving, and furnishings. He was forced to borrow money to get the second outlet going, and the interest absorbed profits and cash flow. As the result of expansion, profits in both locations were lower than the owner had anticipated.

3. *Staffing of a second location is a key factor in achieving success.* The majority of small businesses produce profits at a level directly related to the time the owner puts in. This is true whether or not your labor directly produces profits. A restaurant owner, for example, might succeed primarily because he is a capable and talented cook. How can that be duplicated in a second location? And a consultant sells his or her individual expertise. The challenge, then, is to recruit others with a similar level of expertise to make geographic expansion work.

Example: A goldsmith opened a jewelry store and was successful in selling handmade items. Markup was high and so were profits. But when he considered opening a second location, he realized it simply wouldn't work. The reason for his success was that he used his skill to create merchandise that people wanted to buy. But he was already working at full capacity and selling what he made. A second store could not work because he wouldn't be able to produce enough inventory to meet the market demand.

Even in cases where demand is more than adequate to make expansion successful, growth can be limited by the time you have available. If the continued success of your operation depends on the time *you* put in—as a factor directly influencing sales—then expansion might simply not be possible.

You might be able to train others to duplicate the success you have experienced. But just as a retail clothing store needs a responsible manager to succeed in multiple locations, a handmade jewelry operation, a restaurant, or a consulting enterprise needs talented, well-trained principals to duplicate the owner's talent.

Growing Too Rapidly

You may capitalize expansion well, find capable and responsible managers, delegate and lead effectively, and identify a ready demand. Even so, geographic expansion must still be planned to occur on a methodical schedule. If you attempt to enter new territories too quickly, you will invite a number of management problems you might not be prepared to handle.

Example: The president of a securities brokerage-house wanted to expand beyond his existing five offices in one state. His idea was to open offices all across the country within two years.

This presented a number of problems. In that business, federal and state regulatory agencies impose strict standards on operations and demand close supervision of remote offices. The president, whose background was in the marketing side of the business, understood how to recruit capable salespeople. But he did not appreciate the complexities of the regulatory environment.

Another factor was cost. Expansion would demand a healthy investment in travel, training, legal fees, state licenses and deposits, and compliance expenses. Estimates were that national expansion would cost more than $200,000—just to create new offices. This did not allow for expansion of the home office staff, which would be required to service the remote offices. The president envisioned more than 200 branch offices in forty to forty-five states, and the staff of twelve would not be adequate to respond to requests from the field.

Ultimately, the president achieved his goal. He ended up with 216 offices in forty-four states. However, this took nearly four years and, during that time, the home office staff was increased to about sixty-five people. This expansion demanded considerable management time and maintenance, and the company's profits fell during the expansion period. Problems came up in the compliance area, and the company had to strengthen its supervisory oversight of remote offices. The expansion exercise was successful, but no one had anticipated the full cost of the expansion nor the complexity and time involved in creating it.

Several changes may be necessary for a geographic expansion to work:

- Automated systems for accounting, tax reporting, and payroll
- Larger facilities to house a larger staff
- Hiring of executives and managers to run a more expanded firm

- Regional seminars for training, continuing education, and product updates for a large sales force

Every business has to contend with the complexities that arise from a geographic expansion. Concern for profitability and cash flow are only the surface problems. Of greater concern and demand are the less obvious issues; greater exposure and risk when there are more employees; increased level of permanent overhead; and removal from direct contact with staff, customers, and suppliers.

Growing in the Right Direction

The most important rule of land speculation can be applied to the selection of a business site: The greatest profits are gained by purchasing raw land directly in the path of growth. But to maximize profits, the purchase should be made before anyone else knows the population will grow in that direction.

This key rule demonstrates the risks involved in picking a location, whether it's raw land or a second store. The small-business owner has an advantage over the land speculator, however. You can investigate one or more proposed sites for geographic expansion, and apply several tests to decide which one offers the greatest potential for future profits. You can't completely eliminate the risk, however. The investigation only serves to reduce risk as much as possible.

Here are some guidelines for selecting a second location:

1. *Research the market demand.* Before deciding to invest in a new store, make sure there's a demand for what you are offering. The best way to achieve this is by finding out how many competitors are already there.

For example, suppose you operate a quick-service printing company and are considering opening a second store in the next city. But when you drive around the center of town, you discover that there are already four competing shops within a six square-block area. This leads you to the conclusion that there probably wouldn't be enough business to generate an acceptable margin of profit. You abandon the idea.

2. *Summarize the initial costs.* Just as you prepare a forecast of sales and budget for expenses, you should carefully plan and budget for geographic expansion. This will help you decide whether expansion is a wise move. It will also help you control organizational costs once you proceed with the plan.

In constructing your start-up budget, be sure to include required capital assets, leasehold improvements, lease deposits, and applicable licenses or fees. Also be sure you can afford to cover overhead expenses from inception to the point you anticipate sales will be adequate for you to at least break even. This time period will vary with the type of business, activity at the site, and competition.

3. *Prepare a forecast and budget.* Beyond the start-up budget, also prepare an operating forecast of sales and budget for costs and expenses. This helps determine how long it will take to reach your break-even point and begin producing net profits.

4. *Compare two or more sites during the planning phase.* Good decisions are made through comparison. Don't limit your investigation to just one site. If you're thinking of expanding geographically, apply your tests to two or three regions at the same time. Then go with the one that offers the greatest potential for profit and the shortest period required to recapture your investment.

Comparison of sites might help you decide whether to locate your new shop in a downtown area or in a shopping center. It could also help you identify the total investment required to expand. If the amount is higher than what you can afford, it might be wise to delay your expansion.

5. *Compare resources by region.* In reviewing two or more likely sites for a new shop, compare employee resources. If you plan to hire a manager for the new location, where will you find that person? Will you transfer and promote a current employee or recruit someone new? And how will you supervise the second operation?

These issues will help with the final decision. For example, if you're comparing two sites and one is within ten miles of your home while the other is fifty miles away, what problems would the greater distance bring you? If you transfer an existing employee, will he or she have to commute farther to work? And how much more time will be required for you to travel back and forth to supervise?

Also evaluate potential sites by investigating the likely traffic you'll experience each day. This applies to all retail operations. It helps to watch traffic patterns for a few hours at the proposed site. Look for answers to these questions:

1. What is the average foot-traffic per hour?
2. Is the shop visible to those traveling down the street in their cars?
3. Will traffic be generated from other nearby shops?
4. How many parking spaces are located within one block, and how many competing retail establishments are there?

Based on this information, estimate the number of people you can reasonably expect to visit your store each day. Using historical information (trends from your existing shop), estimate the average sale per walk-in. Use this figure rather than the number of sales actually made; remember, you want to tie the likely foot-traffic to potential daily sales. With these estimates, it's possible to decide whether opening in the new location is feasible. If the site is too small or has too little traffic, you can't realistically expect to turn a profit.

There's a relatively easy test that can help avoid many second-location failures. It involves deciding the level of realistic turnover you can expect to see each month. The turnover rate is the average number of times a full inventory is replaced. It doesn't calculate the full sale of everything on the floor; it only represents an average. Direct costs are divided by the average inventory level to arrive at the number of turns you can expect each month. Based on trends set by your existing store, you then know whether the required number of turns is realistic, based on the number of square feet available for displaying merchandise.

The turnover calculation is shown in Figure 6-1. You summarize your comparative research by completing a worksheet with the estimated results for each proposed new site in Table 6-1.

Quality and Image

You can analyze, study, project, and plan business growth on paper—to the point that you're sure it will work. But once the process is underway, you might discover the real challenge that lies beyond the numbers.

Example: An accountant formed a professional corporation because he was dissatisfied with the impersonal service of large companies. His desire was to work closely with a limited number of clients. The plan worked well for the first three years, but then the accountant considered opening a second office on the other side of town. The plan involved merging the existing business with another

Figure 6-1.   Site evaluation worksheet.

```
 (A) Average sale per
      customer                 $ _____

 (B) Business days per
      month                      _____

 (C) Estimated monthly
      sales (A x B)            $ _____

 (D) Direct costs
      (C x ___ %)             $ _____

 (E) Space available
      for merchandise           _____ sq. ft.

 (F) Cost value of
      inventory               $ _____

 (G) Required turnover
      (D / F)                   _____ times
```

Table 6-1. Regional comparisons.

	Site		
	A	B	C
1. Competitors:			
Number of similar Operations	_____	_____	_____
Distance from site	_____ mi.	_____ mi.	_____ mi.
2. Organizational costs:			
Lease deposits	$_____	$_____	$_____
Rent, 6 months	_____	_____	_____
Improvements	_____	_____	_____
Capital assets	_____	_____	_____
Salaries, 6 months	_____	_____	_____
Other: _____	_____	_____	_____
	_____	_____	_____
Total	$_____	$_____	$_____
3. Budget, six months:			
Sales	$_____	$_____	$_____
Direct costs	_____	_____	_____
Gross profit	$_____	$_____	$_____
Expenses	_____	_____	_____
Net profit	$_____	$_____	$_____

of about the same size, and creating a larger corporation with two principal stockholders.

The plan seemed to make sense, until a more realistic analysis was undertaken. The accountant had limited his first evaluation to a financial test. But even those results were not completely convincing. With twice the receipts, some efficiency could be achieved. However, if the firm had two offices and two staffs, overhead would largely be duplicated. He was forced to realize that, in fact, there would be very little difference between two forms of organization: separate businesses each with their own office, or one business with two outlets. The only significant change would be that each current owner would be exposed to greater risks and responsibilities.

As a result, the accountant decided against expansion. He reminded himself of the original goal: to remain small enough to work closely with a limited number of clients. He was making a good living at current levels, and was in control of all aspects of the operation. Why expand in this case? He risked losing direct contact, thus quality or service as well as his personal reputation could suffer.

Although quality can't be reduced to the black and white of financial analysis, it is a very real factor and must be figured into your geographic-expansion equation. The difficulty is in giving it adequate weight when the other points you want to consider are measurable in terms of dollars and cents. This is one of those decisions you make instinctively, but it's a reality you can't ignore or minimize.

The same is true for personal reputation and image. Many people have broken loose of the corporate life and have started their own business with the purpose of offering more to customers or clients—more in the way of personal attention and service, care and concern, or energy and enthusiasm. Everyone who has started his or her own business knows exactly what that means. A large company with thousands of employees, branch offices, diversified product lines, and corporate reporting chains can't position itself so that the president knows each and every customer. Only an independent business owner can achieve this. And as you expand some of that will be lost.

Example: The owner of a wholesale gift company met with unexpected success and decided to duplicate it on the retail level. He opened a store near his headquarters. Although this was a different merchandising outlet, it was still a second location. Running the wholesale business and one retail store was not an especially difficult chore; the problems began when he opened a second store.

He discovered that delegating day-to-day management was more difficult that he had first thought. Even the most responsible manager failed to exercise the care for merchandising that the owner saw as a priority. Through the wholesale side, the line of products had gained a reputation for high quality, but that was proving difficult to retain with other people involved.

The owner allowed managers to order their own inventory. These managers had retail experience, but did not fully understand the owner's standards for quality merchandising. They tended to order goods that turned over rapidly, and quality and reputation suffered as a result. To fix this problem, the owner restricted the buying trends of store managers. He centralized the inventory and purchasing routines, and imposed strict standards on each store. By taking this control step, he was able to maintain the quality image that had been built up in his wholesale catalog.

Control Over Remote Outlets

The small-business owner needs to control a geographically expanding operation on two levels (see Figure 6-2). First are the financial—cash, inventory, and budgetary—measures meant to ensure that profitability is maintained. Second are the less tangible—your own time, quality of product or service, personal reputation and image—measures that must also be considered.

If you don't control either area, expansion will be an expensive mistake. But with thorough and realistic planning, adequate capitalization, proper timing, and the help of carefully recruited and trained managers and staff, you will gain personal and financial rewards while making your business grow.

Financial Controls

Financial controls include the following:

Figure 6-2. Geographic expansion controls.

```
┌─────────────────────────────────┐
│  A: FINANCIAL                    │
│      1. Cash management          │
│         procedures.              │
│                                  │
│      2. Forecasting and          │
│         budgeting.               │
│                                  │
│      3. Cash-flow planning.      │
│                                  │
│  B: NON–FINANCIAL                │
│      1. Time commitment.         │
│                                  │
│      2. Quality standards.       │
│                                  │
│      3. Customer service.        │
└─────────────────────────────────┘
```

1. *Cash-management procedures.* How can you ensure that cash is correctly managed in a remote location? As long as you are on-site in a single outlet, you have a direct hand in managing the cash. But especially in businesses involving retail sales (those most likely to need expansion for continued growth in profits), a large amount of cash will come through the doors; you must ensure that it is all deposited and accounted for.

The controls you need are exercised in two ways. First is the complete documentation of receipts, through cash-register tapes or numbered invoices. Remember, though, that a clever but dishonest employee can work around your control procedures. While acceptable accounting procedures may be in place, you can't completely guard against theft or embezzlement.

The second method is through analysis of trends. You know from experience the degree of shrinkage you have to expect in a retail operation. Beyond that, analysis of trends in gross profit and inventory levels indicates whether or not all receipts are being accounted for. In a business with large-ticket items, thefts of inventory or cash are difficult to carry off, assuming you are monitoring trends. But when a larger number of items are involved, the theft might be more difficult to discover. You or a responsible administrative manager will have to keep an eye on gross profit trends in order to spot abuse.

2. *Forecasting and budgeting.* You should decide in advance what level of gross income and net profit you will realize in a remote location. Develop a realistic forecast and budget, and communicate your goals to store management. Then review actual results each month, identifying the causes of unfavorable variances.

Budgeting is an essential part of remote outlet management. It's critical even when you spend most of your time in a single location. But budgeting becomes a major source for information as you expand. If unfavorable variances increase, that trend might indicate any number of problems—poor management, negative customer perceptions, theft, or abusive spending, for example—all of which demand immediate action on your part.

You can reverse many of the developing unfavorable trends that take place in an expanding business. This assumes, of course, that you can do two things: you need to know about the trend in the first place; and you must identify the problem and take immediate steps to reverse it. This is where the well-developed budgeting process can be a valuable source of information. Working with accounting and merchandising management professionals in your organization, you can develop the procedures for monitoring trends and then act upon what you discover.

3. *Cash-flow planning.* Even when your business operates profitably, it's possible to suffer serious cash-flow problems. This can result from the need to invest heavily in inventory, outstanding accounts receivable, or capital assets. Or cash-flow problems can definitely arise when expenses are excessive, when gross profit margins disappear owing to theft, or when sales volume is not maintained above the level needed to cover expenses.

You can avoid the problem by proceeding with geographic expansion only when the start-up capital is on hand—without affecting profits and cash flow in the existing outlet. You might need to raise capital through borrowing, with venture capital, or by taking in new partners or stockholders. But those decisions will affect future profits and should be made only after a thorough analysis and revision to the current business plan.

Cash-flow problems are not solved by further expansion. It might be necessary to halt growth long enough to regain control, so your cost margins are established and maintained, and until your expenses are carefully monitored and reduced. In drastic cases, remote locations might have to be closed just to return the company to a position of profitability. You might continue to believe that geographic expansion is a sound idea, however if it's started before you can afford to carry the burden with existing capital, cutting back and waiting for the right moment is a smarter move.

Expansion does not have to occur continously, and reversing the trend often is the only way to stay in business.

Example: The owner of an office-supply company invested money in doubling his inventory and opening a second store. However, accounts receivable rose and sales volume in the second location was not adequate to produce a profit during the first six months. The owner hoped that volume would pick up and customers would pay their bills on time, however he did not take any immediate action to make this happen. At the end of the first year he was forced to close the second store and absorb a big loss.

Example: An importer had met with success in a West Coast location by dealing in oriental antiques. She wanted to duplicate the experience and opened a second office on the East Coast. However, the market for European antiques was not as active there, and market demand did not produce gross or net profits to her expectations, so the second operation did not thrive. In addition, the separation of 3,000 miles meant both locations suffered without the owner's constant presence. The investment in overhead and inventory was too much of a strain, and the owner realized it was a mistake to expand when she did. She closed the East Coast office, and decided to research the possibility of more gradual expansion at a later time.

Nonfinancial Controls

In the second category—the less tangible factors—the following concerns need to be addressed to ensure successful geographic expansion:

1. *Time commitment.* Even when you know how much hands-on effort is required to make an operation work, it's easy to overlook the need for continuing maintenance. Thus many small-business owners have opened second stores only to regret the move.

You are ready to expand *only* when you have invested the time to make your existing location work. That means that day-to-day operational routines have been delegated, problems of delegation have been resolved, and your commitment is limited to the controls you need to exercise. Opening a second location will place just as much demand on your time as the first one did initially, even if you assume that you're better capitalized by the time you make your expansion move.

Example: The owner of a garden-supply business started a second shop. He realized almost as soon as it was open for business that his time was stretched. It took more than thirty minutes to travel from one shop to the other, an exercise that occurred at least twice a day, and sometimes more. And as problems mounted, he had less time to deal with them; his ability to concentrate declined and the pressure seemed endless. The owner suffered for several months but gradually brought both outlets under control. The level of effort was greater than he'd anticipated, and he abandoned plans to expand beyond the two shops—at least for the immediate future.

2. *Quality standards.* You can afford to expand only when you do not need to sacrifice your standards for quality. If you allow the quality of your product or service to fall, you can count on your competition to take your market away from you—in the same way you did when you started out and were able to out-provide your larger competitors.

Growth that occurs gradually and under controlled conditions is possible if you allow time and concentrate on maintaining the high standards you set when you opened your doors. You can grow without losing that standard, but growth must occur on your terms and with the systems and personnel needed to make it all work.

3. *Customer service.* The best way to build loyalty among your customers or clients is to ensure that personalized service

and response are constant. When customers associate these attributes with your organization, they stay with you. Price competition is an obvious problem for every business. But ultimately, real and sustained growth is achieved by offering better service than your competitors. This applies whether you operate a single location for the rest of your life or end up as one of the largest corporations in the country.

Expanding geographically might be a desirable and natural process, however it also poses a threat. It requires a conscious effort and the creation of a customer-service philosophy, along with volume and multiple locations, to ensure permanent growth.

* * *

As your business expands, you will become exposed to ever-growing competitive forces. This results, not only from a geographic presence, but from the overall size of your operation. In many respects smaller companies hold a competitive edge because they have greater flexibility, are in closer touch with an existing market, and need more limited capital. Chapter 7 explains how competition must be considered when your business grows.

Chapter 7

The Competition Trap

You can learn a lot about successful expansion just by becoming an expert on your competition. You will learn more by watching other small businesses as they go after the same market you serve than by judging your performance based on what the big, national firms are doing. Forget the stereotype of the small business that's unable to grow because the larger company has all the advantages. You should be more concerned with what other small companies are doing.

Your first step is to identify exactly who your real competitors are. You might believe that a larger firm always has an advantage, just because it's better financed and more experienced, or because its identity is more firmly established. Capital and identity are distinct advantages, but they don't always mean you can't compete successfully.

A small, growing company has an advantage over its larger competitor, just by virtue of its size. The small company can react with greater speed to changes in the market; it is more likely to be in direct contact with its customer base; and it has more mobility.

Identifying Your Competition

You cannot ignore the fact that larger companies exist and seek the same customers. However, many small businesses fail to grow because they try to compete on the same terms as larger companies. As this occurs, other small competitors quietly pass them by and win that elusive market share.

Why should your eye be on other small companies? The fact is that a bigger competitor might do certain things better than you can. A larger sales force, well-established territories, and years of experience in addressing the customer's needs are obvious advantages. But big companies also have distinct disadvantages (see Figure 7-1). For example:

1. *Decision making is more complex in larger companies.* Multiple management levels complicate reporting and communication. So the bigger the company, the more difficult it is to act, even on the most basic level.

2. *Decision makers may be far removed from the customer.* Decision makers often spend most of their time meeting with other executives. The higher up executives are on the chain of command, the more insulated they are from the customer. In contrast, you probably see your customers on a regular basis.

3. *A decision in a large company often depends on issues far beyond the immediate question.* The pressures on executives of big companies are intensified by a vast array of considerations. These include considering the interests of stockholders, the board of directors, and hundreds—if not thousands—of em-

Figure 7-1. Large competitor disadvantages.

1. **Complexity of decision-making.**

2. **Distance from the customer.**

3. **Multiple decision issues.**

4. **Lack of direct experience.**

5. **Inability to move quickly.**

ployees. So what is a relatively simple decision for a small company can be very complex one in a bigger company.

4. *Top management might have little or no actual experience in running a particular type of organization.* Diversified companies are often run by people who don't have a lot of experience managing the subsidiaries in their charge. The hard lesson many big operations have learned is that a successful formula in one type of business doesn't always lead to success in another.

5. *Timing is on the side of the smaller competitor.* You have a distinct advantage over your larger competitor in the fact that a small business is more agile and flexible. You're still defining your organization. Big companies, by their nature, need rigid procedures and rules, strict reporting chains, and inflexible response systems.

The large company is certainly going to maintain some market share. But that doesn't mean you can't find a different customer base of your own, especially one that the big company can't address. Larger companies can't tailor themselves to a specific market as well as you can. In that respect, the larger operation is not competing for *your* market. Companies of similar size or smaller are of more immediate concern. Identify your method of competing, based on the guidelines given in Figure 7-2 and in greater detail here:

Figure 7-2.   Guidelines: competing effectively.

1. **Concentrate on a few strengths.**

2. **Give the customer clear service comparisons.**

3. **Create your own timetable.**

4. **Focus on your best market.**

1. *Concentrate on a few strengths, rather than trying to move too rapidly.* What do you offer that other companies do not? Or what can you do better? Pay attention to where other small companies are headed. How do you define *excellence* for your customer? How do you set yourself apart? Ask this, not in comparison to a larger firm, but with regard to other small firms.

Example: The owner of a regional securities firm screened salespeople diligently, hiring only those with a track record of generating high volume *and* with demonstrated professional integrity. The owner was tempted to expand the number of branch offices, but he knew he couldn't compete with Dean Witter and Shearson. So instead of chasing that market, the owner concentrated on overcoming the flaws associated with the smaller firm: lack of service after the sale, high turnover among the sales force, and offering so many services that nothing is done well.

2. *Give the customer an easy way to make a service comparison.* Identify the common weaknesses of your competition and use those weaknesses to market your services. Don't promise what you can't deliver, in an attempt to shut down the competition.

Example: The owner of a computer-hardware sales company sold products manufactured by larger companies. Other stores in the area were selling the same products. She noticed, though, that customers had two big problems. First, they weren't getting the sales support they needed to make an informed decision. In particular, salespeople weren't trained to educate customers who might know very little about computers. Second, when hardware broke down, customers did not get prompt repair service from the store where they purchased the equipment. The owner competed very successfully by offering exceptional service in both areas. Salespeople were thoroughly trained to work with customers at the point of sale. And the owner invested money in building a repair service for the products she sold. In this way, she competed well with other small operations.

3. *Create your own timetable, and don't make your decisions based on what the competition is doing.* Expansion should occur

only when you are prepared, and as dictated by your business plan. In too many instances, growing companies forget their objective and their plan, and make decisions based on how the competition acts.

Example: The owner of an antique store planned to add more stores in the future. However, she first wanted to concentrate on building a reputation in one store, where her daily presence ensured good customer service and quality products. But when a direct competitor opened a second store, she decided to follow suit. Expansion was premature, and the second store did not thrive. To make matters worse, sales in the first store eroded, and it took many months to get the operation back on track.

4. *Focus on your best market, not just on what's assumed to be the only market.* The market you're best suited to sell to might be defined beyond the generally assumed market. Look beyond what everyone believes the market to be. What does the customer want and need? How can you offer it? You will serve a different customer than the one who goes to a large national firm, and perhaps you will find a specialization that other, smaller competitors have not yet discovered.

Example: A contractor competed for several years in two markets. He placed bids on big projects, but won very few because larger firms were able to outbid him. And those he did win were marginally profitable; on some, he even lost money. The other market was for residential repair work, which demanded a high advertising budget and limited repeat business. Finally, the contractor identified the market he was best suited to go after: major home improvements. In his region, many homeowners preferred renovation over moving, and activity was on the increase. The repair-service companies in the area were not addressing this market, since their emphasis was on smaller-scale jobs. And the very large firms were busy putting up new housing developments, shopping centers, and industrial parks. The contractor discovered a profitable market, and soon became the major competitor in that specialization.

Myths About Competition

You can identify your own competition trap by examining the popular myths, and then questioning how you can find your own best market. These include:

1. *The competition is an elusive, unknown factor.* There is really nothing mysterious about your competition. Other companies face the same problems and decisions. The difference in success arises from the way you deal with competitive factors. If you are faced with a tough marketing decision today, you can count on one thing: your competitors are wrestling with the same problem.

As long as you keep this in mind, you will gain a competitive advantage by anticipating the future and minimizing risks. It's a mistake to try and outguess the competition, to make a move before "they" do. Pursue the course that's best for you, as dictated by your marketing plan and your objective.

2. *You must be prepared to meet the competition head on.* This implies that only the strong survive, and that there's only room for one successful company in any given market. But in fact you don't survive by trying to crush your competitors, or by meeting them in a direct confrontation. You survive by concentrating on what's best for you. Instead of preparing yourself for a clash, move around your competition. Identify your own market.

3. *The faster you expand, the stronger your competitive position.* This fallacy has trapped a number of small businesses. Expansion is motivated, not by timing or a well-conceived plan, but by fear that the competition will get there first. Remember, expanding too rapidly weakens your competitive stance and makes you more vulnerable. Leave rapid expansion ventures to other companies, and take a more methodical, controlled course.

4. *Competition is bad for you.* In truth, competition is a positive factor. You can judge your expansion program partly by watching your competitors. What are they doing differently, and what are the results? Where have they failed, and how can you avoid the same mistakes? How have they succeeded, and how can you imitate that success? Perhaps the most valuable information you can learn from the competition is what the customer wants that the competition is not giving them. That information tells you specifically how to expand successfully.

If you have no competition, does that mean you "own" the market? It might seem so at first glance. A demand for something exists, and there's only one place to get it. But if you don't have any competitors, be aware of two points. First, without competitors you have no means for comparison. How do you know your service level is acceptable? How can you judge demand? How can you measure customer response? Second, if there is a demand for what you sell the lack of competition is only a temporary condition. Invariably, someone else will see that you're the only game in town and will challenge your market position. If you're asleep at the wheel, the younger, hungrier competitor will soon pass you by and take away your market.

This latter situation is perhaps the greatest competition trap. You spend time and effort building a strong market position, either as the only company offering a product or as the best. Then, once you've achieved that growth plateau, you relax and coast along. It might be the biggest myth of all to believe that once the competition is eliminated (or if it simply doesn't yet exist) the game has been won. That's when you're in the most vulnerable position of all.

What You Need to Know

Knowing as much as possible about your competition is the best way to maintain your market share. That means you should compare yourself to other companies, constantly. What do you hear from your customers about their quality, service, and pricing? How does your response compare to what the competition is doing?

Follow the guidelines shown in Figure 7-3 and listed here to stay in touch with competitors:

1. *Read their advertising and promotional literature regularly.* Become a student of your competition. Don't assume that you can't learn anything from the methods your competitor uses. Expose yourself to all their advertisements, including what they have in the phone book, in newspapers, on the radio, and

Figure 7-3.   Guidelines: knowing the competitor.

1. **Read their advertisements and promotional literature regularly.**

2. **Ask your customers what they think.**

3. **Learn from your competitors' successes – and from their mistakes.**

4. **Compare sales and service formulas.**

5. **Meet the competing management directly.**

on television. Get copies of their brochures, pamphlets, newsletters, and other printed materials.

How do the competition's promotional activities compare to yours? Do they advertise more extensively? What promises do they make? Are they able to keep their promises? What is their strongest and weakest point, and how can you use that information to improve your own advertising?

2. *Ask your customers what they think.* Stay in touch with your customers. Ask them how your service compares to what the competition offers. There are good reasons why people stay with you or go to the other side. Some of your customers buy from more than one source, and you can find out why by asking. Use direct contact, conduct surveys, or include questions on initial contact literature.

3. *Learn from your competitors' successes—and from their mistakes.* It's not enough to gather information. You must also be prepared to respond, to change your strategies based on what you find. If customers tell you that they buy from the competitor because its service is better, that tells you where you need to make changes. If the competitor's advertising makes a promise that you don't make, ask yourself: Can it deliver on its promise? Can I promise more? Can I deliver?

Also look for mistakes the competition makes, and learn from those mistakes. If another company promises the lowest price and the most responsive service, does it come through? Failing to deliver on a promise is a deadly mistake—one the customer doesn't forget. Be cautious in the promises you make. If you succeed, you'll build customer loyalty; if you fail, the customer will never trust you again.

4. *Compare sales and service formulas.* Companies grow when they focus on a specific market, address a clear demand, and come through on their promises. What does the competition offer? What formula have they discovered?

Imagine this situation. For the last two years, your company has been growing at a healthy pace. But this year, a new company has entered the market, and it's taking a good share of your market. Your own growth rate has slowed. Why? How does the competitor appeal to the customer, and why is the response going that way? Is it a matter of price, service, or quality? If you guarantee two-day delivery for $35, and the competitor promises one-day delivery for no charge, should you change your policy? Or should you emphasize lower price, better after-sale service, or a wider range of products? By knowing the competition's formula you can identify your next move. That formula isn't necessarily better, but it does point the way to change your own emphasis.

5. *Meet the competing management directly.* You might discover that your major competitor is not a competitor at all. While your ads might sound the same, and customers might appear to be the same people, significant differences could save you and your competitor a lot of energy and effort.

For example, suppose you own a marketing consultation business, and a new consulting firm recently opened its doors in your area. Call the owner and set up a lunch meeting. Find out exactly what kinds of clients it seeks and services it offers. If you are direct competitors, you will soon find out. But if you address different markets, it may be an advantage for both of you to be aware of one another. The competitor might become a source for referrals or, at the very least, might not pose a threat to your market at all.

Building Customer Loyalty

Most of the lessons you learn about competition come from other companies in the same market. In many respects, larger companies—by virtue of their size—are not in the same market as you. But you can learn one critical lesson from larger competitors—the importance of customer loyalty.

Successful large companies are built on a foundation of loyal customers. That doesn't come about just because a company advertises heavily, has outlets in every major city, or has been around for fifty years. Customer loyalty is the outgrowth of tangible and prompt response to demand, both at the point of sale and after the sale.

Permanent and successful expansion occurs when you also create that loyalty. But you do better to create a solid relationship with one loyal customer than sell to five customers who may not return—or who are dissatisfied.

Promising service and then delivering it is an investment in your own future. Consider the many large stores that advertise their policy for returns, for example. You can return merchandise and receive a refund, no questions asked. As long as the store continues to deliver on that promise, a core of loyal customers will always be there. Even if customers are never dissatisfied with the merchandise they buy, they know the store's reputation and they depend on it.

In comparison, if a merchant argues with the customer or refuses to give a refund, that ensures that the customer will never come back. Even worse, it creates a negative reputation, one that will ultimately prevent the success the owner wants.

The formula is very simple:

> Promise your customer more than the competition promises, and then deliver what you promise—without exception.

As your operation expands, this simple formula becomes more difficult to maintain. That's why expansion has to be controlled and timed carefully. While you're at the helm of a single outlet, you can review every customer contact directly and put your policies into action. Response is swift and consistent. But when you open a second location, that all-important response is delegated. The idea of making and keeping a promise to the customer should be the key element of your objective, and it should be the highest priority for all your employees.

As your competitors expand, chances are their service commitment will begin to fail. This unfortunate consequence of growth presents a clear lesson: If you make a promise you must be able to come through, every time and for every customer. And if expansion means that you're not sure the promise is still valid, then you're not ready to expand.

Only when you are certain that your employees respect and understand the service commitment can you go forward and succeed. You will build customer loyalty when the formula works equally well in multiple outlets, for multiple product or service lines, or when your management task has been delegated to other people.

Many businesses have discovered a successful formula and have attempted to expand it, only to discover that they are unable—now at a greater size—to build loyalty among their customer base. That's when the smaller, more diligent competitor enters and takes over. That's probably how you started your business. Don't make the same mistake larger competitors make: failing to recognize the power of a smaller, more aware company looking for a gap to fill.

Expansion and Competitive Factors

A small, new business operating on a shoestring might be awed by the might of its larger competitors. But the owner of such a company soon recognizes the gap between demand and response, and is able to fill that gap to create a winning formula. The competition trap shows up somewhere between being very small and very large. The company that has grown to a plateau where the market is strong and a specific demand is being met also finds itself on the verge of falling into the competition trap.

At this point, your business is no longer the new company on the block, and you might not be the aggressive, aware owner with a point of view forgotten or overlooked by others. Instead, you're in danger of becoming the entrenched, larger competitor—the target for everyone else moving along the growth track.

The following guidelines for keeping your point of view fresh and for maintaining your focus are listed in Figure 7-4.

1. *Always put the customer first—even if it means losing money.* One reason many small businesses remain small is that the owners are more concerned with immediate profits than with building a long-term relationship with their customers. The dockets of small claims courts provide many examples. Customers ask for refunds and business owners refuse. In many of these cases, the owner might win a $30 dispute, but he or she loses the customer for life.

If you put the customer first, even when you have the legal right to say no, you build a permanent and loyal customer base. Even if that means losing a sale unjustly, it's worth the price. Assume that every customer will come back if you honor even an implied promise. The satisfied customer is your best advertisement; the dissatisfied ex-customer goes just as far in establishing a negative reputation.

2. *Never stop watching your competition—on all sides.* It's a mistake to set the tone of your business based only on what

Figure 7-4. Competitive guidelines.

1. **Always put the customer first.**

2. **Never stop watching your competition.**

3. **Think of yourself as the underdog.**

4. **Work from your objective.**

the industry leader is doing. The big national companies have grown to their current size over many years, and they don't face the same competitive challenges you face. Watch the big companies, but also watch the smaller ones. Look for signs of emerging companies that have identified gaps in what *you* offer, while at the same time watching for gaps left by others.

3. *Think of yourself as the underdog, no matter how much success you achieve.* Never become overconfident or too relaxed in your success, and never settle for achieving a particular plateau of growth. Remember that there's always someone else waiting for you to become complacent. The underdog is keenly aware of the competition, and looks for every advantage. As long as you think of yourself in that role, you can maintain a sharp focus, be ready to respond when opportunities are presented, and build permanent growth.

4. *Work from your objective, not someone else's.* Respond to signals from your customers and always remember your objective, especially how you define excellence. As long as you concentrate on building *your* market at the most suitable pace, you won't go wrong. But if you abandon your plan because the competition is moving in a new direction, that's when the problems begin.

*   *   *

A healthy, realistic attitude about your competition is one way to measure how well you're achieving your planned growth. When combined with the other tests of expansion, you will be able to control the rate and quality of growth. And that must be measured. Ultimately, when all of the methods of expansion are reviewed collectively, your success will be evaluated in terms of profit and loss. And that's the subject of the next chapter.

III
SOLUTIONS

Chapter 8

Valid Scorekeeping

Financial information is essential as a tracking tool and as a means for measuring success. The statements and account analyses prepared from your books can point out emerging trends and help you prevent financial catastrophe. Forecasting and budgeting techniques define your goals in financial terms, and help you reach them. And the judgments others make concerning your net worth and success will most likely be based strictly on financial information.

Properly used, financial data provide a tangible and consistent measurement of your operation. But in fact, the numbers—as critical as they are—represent only half of the success equation. The other half consists of the less tangible standards you've expressed in your business objective: rules concerning product and service quality, and desired relations with employees, customers, and suppliers.

Combining Financial and Nonfinancial Tests

The real bottom line for your business cannot be restricted to isolated measurements of profit and loss. In practice, you are better able to judge expansion with a combination of financial and nonfinancial tests. In fact, your ability to expand successfully is determined largely by how well you coordinate the tangibles seen in financial results and the intangibles of your objective. That combination determines the degree of control you will maintain during periods of expansion.

Example: A very successful retail operation grew steadily over many years, adding a new store on average every eighteen months. The capital was available to fund rapid expansion, but the owner took time to ensure that internal controls were in place, and that her own time was used properly. The standard for growth was tied to quality and internal control, without exception.

Example: A management-consulting firm found unexpected demand in the market, and took on many more clients than the owner was prepared for. At the end of the second year, gross income was more than twice the amount forecast. But the owner's time was no longer within his own control. He didn't want to work sixty hours a week, but that's what the schedule demanded. He was unable to control the course of the operation or the use of his own time—his primary reasons for going into business and, he realized, with very high priority.

Example: The owner of a toy manufacturing company was very successful in marketing a limited line of handmade products of exceptional quality. Growing market demand offered the potential for rapid expansion into new product lines, but the owner resisted. He asked these three questions:

1. Will we still be able to produce handmade products of exceptional quality? Or will we have to trade quality for volume?
2. What market are we in? Does expansion mean moving away from the reputation we've built so carefully over the past few years?
3. If we're able to expand, what actions will I need to take to ensure that quality does not suffer?

Invariably, the answers to these questions led to acceptance of a slower rate of expansion than the numbers indicated would be possible. Placing a high priority on quality made all the difference.

Expansion may be allowed to occur at an appropriate rate. It doesn't mean expansion is impossible. The numbers don't lie; they may indicate that the time is right and that the opportunity is there. But they don't tell the whole story, either. Even with opportunities for expansion, every decision should be made in the context of your company's objective.

Financial Tests

What financial tests are most valuable during periods of expansion? Many small-business owners attempt to conduct a financial review only by looking over the monthly or quarterly financial statements: balance sheet, income statement, and statement of cash flows. These traditional reports give you a valuable broad overview, but you need more. Following are other financial tests you should put to work during periods of expansion.

Sales Forecast

One of the most dependable financial tests is the sales forecast. The straightforward way to measure expansion is in terms of gross sales, forecast six to twelve months ahead. In fact, you really can't predict cost and expense levels unless you have first estimated future sales.

A sales forecast should be constructed on the basis of reasonable assumptions. If you depend on a sales force for revenues, base your forecast on recruitment goals, average production per person, and planned territorial expansion. Historical information is useful in planning future volume. If you sell directly to the public through retail outlets, base your assumptions on planned new stores and historical growth curves of existing stores—with an awareness of demand limits in each location. And if you sell a service, base your forecast on available service hours, existing and new contracts, and realistic demand levels.

The sales forecast is constructed on a series of assumptions. For example, a company that sells through field representatives might make the following set of assumptions:

1. During the year, we will recruit a total of thirty-nine new salespeople, on this schedule:

Jan	2	May	4	Sep	4
Feb	4	Jun	2	Oct	2
Mar	3	Jul	4	Nov	4
Apr	4	Aug	3	Dec	3
				Total	39

2. The existing sales force of 107 people will decline by an average of one person per month, owing to resignations and terminations.
3. Average production generated by salespeople who have been with the company one year or less will be $3,200 per month; for those with the company more than one year, monthly production will average $6,900. These estimates are based on historical averages.

The forecast is built by translating each of the assumptions into actual amounts. The value of documenting this process so carefully will be seen later, when you want to compare actual results to the forecast. To know what action to take when variances are discovered, you need to compare average production and recruitment to your earlier assumptions. Only then will you know how to keep your expansion plan on course. By comparing actual to assumed recruitment levels and average production, you can identify exact causes and, from that, decide on exact actions to correct discovered problems.

Table 8-1 shows the actual forecast built from the assumptions just mentioned.

The sales forecast should be developed with your objective in mind, not just from what you assume to be the maximum rate of increase. That's the most common flaw in forecasting. Don't always project the maximum if, in fact, you don't want your business to grow at top speed. Ask yourself what a manageable level is and how much growth you want to *allow* to happen this year. These are different questions from the

Table 8-1. Sales forecast.

	Existing		New		
	Number of		*Number of*		
Month	*Sales*	*Amount*	*Sales*	*Amount*	*Total*
Jan	107	$ 738,300	2	$ 6,400	$ 744,700
Feb	106	731,400	6	19,200	750,600
Mar	105	724,500	9	28,800	753,300
Apr	104	717,600	13	41,600	759,200
May	103	710,700	17	54,400	765,100
Jun	102	703,800	19	60,800	764,600
Jul	101	686,900	23	73,600	770,500
Aug	100	690,000	26	83,200	773,200
Sep	99	683,100	30	96,000	779,100
Oct	98	676,200	32	102,400	778,600
Nov	97	669,300	36	115,200	784,500
Dec	96	662,400	39	124,800	787,200
Total		$8,404,200		$806,400	$9,210,600

ones more often asked, namely, "What's the most growth I can achieve, and what *might* occur if everything goes my way?"

Cost and Expense Budget

A second valuable financial tool is the cost and expense budget. This should be prepared only after settling on a sales forecast, because sales levels will affect many categories of expense and all categories of direct cost.

The budget is built in a way similar to the forecast: assumptions serve as the basis for estimating an account's future level. Assumptions may be historically based or modified with new information, such as:

- Vendors' current prices
- Assumed price increases
- Price savings from changing vendors

Some budgets should be based on the number of employees. For example, if you have budgeted for staff additions, you may also need to locate larger office space. Accounts such as telephone, travel, and office supplies may be affected by changes in staff levels.

Use a form such as the one shown in Figure 8-1 to document assumptions and create budgets for all accounts. This form leaves space for as many as three components making up the contents of an account. For example, you might break "Printing Expense" into three groups: forms, letterhead, and

Figure 8-1.   Assumption worksheet.

Account _____ Year _____				
MONTH	1	2	3	TOTAL

EXPLANATION

1 _____

_____

_____

2 _____

_____

_____

3 _____

_____

_____

business cards. Or "Office Supplies" could consist of breakdowns by supplier or by type of supply. When necessary, worksheets should be attached to your assumption worksheet so that every assumption is completely explained.

The "explanation" space at the bottom of the form is used to show how an assumption was made. The explanation may involve a calculation based on historical levels, a known price increase or reduction, the number of employees, or the level of sales.

Cash-Flow Projections

You might reach your sales forecast goals and even stay within your cost and expense budget for the year. But during an expansion phase, one of the biggest chronic problems is deterioration of cash flow. You want to ensure that the rate of growth is controlled so that working capital is available to pay your current bills.

Problems arise when growing companies invest too much capital in inventory or capital assets, when expense levels outpace the rate of sales, and when outstanding receivable balances are allowed to climb too high.

Your cash-flow projection is a tool for monitoring cash availability. It starts with an assumption about the level of profit (forecast sales minus budgeted costs and expenses). This figure is then increased by the amount of depreciation you have budgeted, since that's a noncash expense, and adjusted for estimates of:

- Payments on outstanding loans
- Increases in inventory or accounts receivable
- Investment in capital assets
- Amounts you plan to draw out of the business

Plan your cash flow using a worksheet like the one shown in Figure 8-2. Each month's ending balance is carried forward and becomes the next month's beginning balance. Be aware that during an expansion you can report a healthy profit and still run into cash-flow problems. The purpose of the projection

Figure 8-2.   Cash-flow projections.

	MONTH:	MONTH:	MONTH:
Beginning balance			
Plus:			
Net profit			
Depreciation			
Cash–basis profit			
Plus:			
Loan proceeds			
Sale of fixed assets			
Total			
Less:			
Increase in inventory			
Increase in receivables			
Increase in capital assets			
Owner draws			
Loan payments			
Total			
Ending balance			

worksheet is to create guidelines and then monitor and control cash balances.

The sales forecast, cost and expense budget, and cash-flow projection represent the budgeting process. They are valuable *only* if you compare actual results to the budgets every month, and then take the actions indicated by the variances that show up. If you do not act to correct discovered variances, the entire budgeting exercise is just that—an exercise.

Description: You discover that sales are falling below the level you forecast. A comparison shows that you are recruiting fewer new people than you anticipated.

Solution: Catch up with recruitment goals as expressed in your plan, and make up the difference in future months.

Description: A monthly review shows that travel expenses are exceeding the budgeted level. You determine that the reason is lack of an approval procedure. Managers are charging travel expenses without comparing costs and without preapproval.

Solution: Put one employee in charge of investigating fares, and institute a procedure for preapproval of all travel expenses.

Description: Your cash-flow projection did not anticipate an increase in average levels of outstanding accounts receivable.

Solution: Delegate responsibility for contacting past due accounts and speeding up the rate of collections.

Cash-Flow Analysis

While your business is expanding, you are in constant danger of experiencing cash-flow problems. Using the cash-flow projection to monitor ongoing trends is a necessary financial step. Beyond this, keep a close eye on two areas: receivables and inventory. These apply to all businesses that allow customers or clients to accumulate balances each month, or that buy materials and keep inventory on hand.

Control of cash flow during an expansion phase is critical. Some small-business owners assume that expansion will solve cash-flow problems when, in fact, it usually accelerates them. Expansion works only when you pay close attention to your cash status.

Analyze collections by tracking the payment trends from one month to the next. Summarize the time each outstanding account has been on the books, using an aging list like the one shown in Figure 8-3. This form enables you to review the status of all accounts each month. The summary shows the portion that is current (from zero to thirty days), and at each stage of past due. The older the outstanding balance, the less likelihood it will be collected. If you allow an ever-growing portion of receivables to move into the past-due columns, you will experience a corresponding cash-flow problem.

One limitation of this list is that it reviews the past. For situations in which collections are a chronic problem, it might be necessary to review aging status every week, place limits on

Figure 8-3.   Aging list.

NAME	TOTAL	DAYS OUTSTANDING			
		0–30	31–60	61–90	OVER

SUMMARY	
0–30	_____ %
31–60	_____
61–90	_____
OVER	_____
	100.0%

the dollar amount customers are allowed to accumulate each month, and prevent further charges until older balances have been paid in full.

Besides carefully monitoring trends in accounts receivable, watch inventory levels. Make sure that:

• You are not overinvesting in inventory.

- Inventory controls are in place.
- Purchasing and shipping records are complete.

There is a fine distinction between maintaining an adequate inventory and overinvesting. You can test the adequacy of inventory levels by using the inventory turnover ratio, a comparison between the cost of goods sold and average inventory levels. This ratio is explained later in this chapter.

Key Account Analysis

Owners of small businesses sometimes dismiss the value of account analysis as a bureaucratic procedure, one practiced only in large companies. That would be true if the analysis forms were completed and then filed without review or response. And if you analyze too many accounts, the process becomes a burden, both to your staff (in the demands of preparation time) and for you (in review time).

Certain key accounts should be analyzed every month, including:

- *Cash*—analyzed through the bank reconciliation and monitored by signature and approval control procedures.
- *Accounts Receivable*—balanced between the general ledger and your subsidiary accounts.
- *Inventory*—balanced by comparisons among requisitions, shipping and receiving records, and physical counts.
- *Accounts Payable*—balanced by reversal of monthly accruals and correct posting to cost and expense accounts.
- *Other Asset and Liability Accounts*—analyzed and reconciled depending on the volume of transactions, nature of the account, and difficulty in past attempts at identifying balances.

As a general rule, your accountant or bookkeeper should analyze each asset and liability account, and be able to fully account for all balances. In addition, any cost or expense account needing special controls should be analyzed and monitored regularly.

Each account-analysis form should be tailored to suit the account; no one form will work in all cases. Use blank worksheets to set up the monthly analyses, so you can reconcile and explain the balances in each asset and liability account or summarize the activity in a cost or expense account.

Ratio and Trend Tests

A number of ratios can be used to test the trends at work in your expanding company. Circumstances will dictate which of these is of most value and whether additional tests should be devised and used. Ratios are useful only when reviewed in comparison. They represent the latest entry in a trend, and should be considered in that light.

Here are five of the more common ratios that test working capital (see also Figure 8-4). In addition to these, a wide number of ratios can be applied to evaluate sales, cost and expense levels, and the relationship between specific accounts. This is a brief coverage, intended to show the tools for trend analysis that will be most useful during expansion periods.

1. *Current Ratio.* This compares current assets with current liabilities. As a general rule, this ratio should be maintained at a 2 to 1 or higher level, indicating healthy control over working capital.

Example: Current assets (cash, accounts receivable, and inventory) total $192,800. Current liabilities (payable within one year) are $87,600. The current ratio is:

$$\frac{192,800}{87,600} = 2.2 \text{ to } 1$$

2. *Quick Assets Ratio.* This is similar to the current ratio, but inventory is excluded. As a general rule, this ratio should be maintained at a 1 to 1 or higher level.

Figure 8-4. Working capital ratios.

A: CURRENT RATIO

$$\frac{current\ assets}{current\ liabilities} = x\ to\ 1$$

B: QUICK ASSETS RATIO

$$\frac{current\ assets - inventory}{current\ liabilities} = x\ to\ 1$$

C: TURNOVER IN WORKING CAPITAL

$$\frac{current\ assets - current\ liabilities}{net\ sales} = x\ turns$$

D: INVENTORY TURNOVER

$$\frac{cost\ of\ goods\ sold}{average\ inventory} = x\ turns$$

E: DEBT/EQUITY RATIO

$$\frac{liabilities}{net\ worth} = x\ \%$$

Example: Current assets (cash, accounts receivable, and inventory) total $92,800. Current liabilities (those payable within one year) are $87,600. The current ratio is:

$$\frac{92,800}{87,600} = 1.1\ to\ 1$$

3. *Turnover in Working Capital.* This ratio shows how many times, on average, working capital was used (or turned) to produce the volume of sales. Working capital is the difference between current assets and current liabilities. Net sales are divided by working capital.

Example: Current assets as of the end of the year total $192,800. Current liabilities are $87,600. Net sales for the year are $843,600. Turnover in working capital is:

$$\frac{843,600}{192,800 - 87,600} = 8.0 \text{ turns}$$

4. *Inventory Turnover.* This is a measurement of the number of times, on average, inventory was replaced during the year. Like the previous measurement of turnover, it does not represent actual replacement, but only an average. The cost of goods sold for the year is divided by the average inventory level.

This ratio can be used to judge how consistently you maintain inventory levels, so that you do not invest an excessive amount of capital in merchandise, thus affecting cash flow.

Example: The cost of goods sold for the year is $502,800. Average inventory level is $107,000. The inventory turnover:

$$\frac{502,800}{107,000} = 4.7 \text{ turns}$$

5. *Debt/Equity Ratio.* This ratio compares the level of debt capital to total capital, for the purpose of identifying movement in debt and equity. Total liabilities (debts) are divided by net worth.

Maintaining a consistent level between debt and equity, or managing to reduce the debt level over time, will help control cash flow. If interest expense is allowed to rise over time because you increase debt, that will reduce profits. And at the same time, a growing level of principal payments will further deteriorate working capital.

Example: Total debts as of the end of the year are $147,800. Total net worth is $315,000. The debt/equity ratio:

$$\frac{147,800}{315,000} = 46.9\%$$

The explanation of account analysis and ratios is a broad overview only. The tests should be based on the nature of your business, the rate of expansion, and the scope of your operating budget. Consult with your accountant to identify the ratios and trend tests that will best help you monitor and control your rate of expansion.

Monitoring financial information during expansion can be viewed as a controlled reconciliation between your plan and the actual results, on three levels: objective, plan, and budget. Each level represents an area of conflict between what you expect and what actually occurs.

You would never expect the year's outcome to match your forecast and budget; that's not the purpose of the budgeting procedure. The same rule applies when you compare your objective to the market opportunities; you will not always want to follow every avenue that presents itself. And just because circumstances arise that you could exploit, it does not mean you should veer from a well-conceived plan.

When you combine financial tests with the standards set by your business objective, you improve the review process and sharpen your focus. You know which outcomes help the expansion plan, and which ones might harm it; and you are able to control the rate and timing of expansion. In other words, you're running things by your own rules.

The following three levels requiring reconciliation are shown in Figure 8-5. As further explanation, consider the goals of each step:

Figure 8-5.   Expectation and outcome.

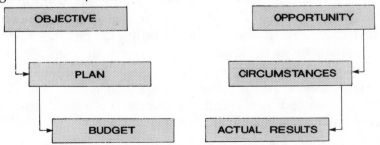

Expectation	Outcome
Objective—defines standards and reasons you are in business	**Opportunity**—arises for expansion outside of the objective
Plan—defines the steps you intend to take this year	**Circumstances**—may affect your plan or lead you to alter it
Budget—imposes standards and estimates for outcome, used as a measurement of actual results	**Actual results**—point the way to required control measures or budgeting flaws

Scorekeeping Flaws

Ratios are tracked over a period of months and changes in trends are studied. Here is an example. If a key ratio consistently falls within a narrow range and then suddenly moves beyond that range, the change is a signal. By examining the causes, you will discover what important element has changed, and that will lead you to the appropriate response. Your response may be to tighten a procedure, pull back on expansion, improve controls, or revise the plan.

Financial information provides you with clear, exact indicators. During periods of expansion, however, be aware that the numbers by themselves are not the only valid tests. As companies grow, it's easy to fall into the trap of paying attention only to financial information, for several reasons:

1. *Financial results can be measured precisely and consistently.* This is an advantage when financial results are coordinated with your objective. But the same feature can become the source of trouble. It's reassuring to be able to measure results in comparison to the past, to an acceptable norm, or to a budget and forecast. Compared to other, less tangible tests, the facts are easily measured. It's easy to ignore the other tests you should apply and the questions you should constantly ask.

2. *Numbers are the accepted standard for judging success or failure.* Success in business is most often defined in financial

terms. It's not enough simply to earn a profit; traditional thinking states that a business has succeeded only if sales are higher this year than the year before; if territories grew; and if a company hired more employees. Unfortunately, these common tests ignore one important point: In spite of the way a company's success is judged, the best rate of expansion might not conform to this definition of success.

Because there may be a conflict between the usual method of judging results and your own best rate of expansion, you are under constant pressure to force growth. You may come to believe that expansion is necessary for the company to remain a "successful" operation, even if you know it's not ready for it.

3. *It's naturally assumed that a business desires expansion and higher profits—right now.* Ask most owners if they'd like to see more sales next year, and they'll answer, "Of course, who wouldn't?" You also want to grow, but at a rate you can monitor and control. The widely accepted standard might not apply to you, at least not this year. In some cases you will be more successful by delaying expansion and consolidating your gains to this point. As an alternative, consider this rule:

> Expansion and higher profits are desirable, but only at a manageable rate, and only when the time is right.

4. *Small-company trends are judged by the same standards as applied to large companies.* It's a mistake to measure your company's performance next to the results of a large, national company. However, common standards for financial success are usually applied to all companies, regardless of size. A big company might have the capital and other resources to manage substantial growth, while your own rate of expansion can occur only within the constraints of a limited capital budget. Your financial standards should not be the same as those applied to large companies.

Getting the Facts

It's important to let your employees know exactly what you want in the way of financial information. Your ability to monitor and control the rate of expansion depends on timely and accurate financial information. Although financial reporting is a precise and consistent process, the interpretation of numbers can vary considerably. Accounting standards allow wide latitude in the timing and interpretation of results.

What this means is that you might receive very different reports from two or more people, depending on their interpretation of the numbers and also based on their perception of what you *want* to hear. You can't afford to look only for good news, or to allow positive interpretations that make results seem better than they are. What you want are the facts—both good and bad.

Example: The owner of a growing marketing company wanted monthly reports on sales activity, expense budgets, and profits. However, these reports showed no negatives in recent months. The owner realized that, in order for the reports to serve a useful purpose, they must be revised so that problems could be spotted. He asked his bookkeeper to revise the reports so he could compare sales activity to forecast levels, track actual expenses next to the budget, and look for solutions to any negative variances.

You can't afford to let the usual or traditional standards of financial review take over. If that occurs, your objective becomes insignificant and the company evolves into something other than what you conceived, moving at its own speed, in its own direction, and without any direct leadership.

Setting Individual Standards

Establish reasonable and useful standards for interpreting your operation's financial results, beyond the traditional methods. Here are some guidelines:

1. *Review the numbers with the objective and the plan constantly in mind.* When your financial report shows that actual sales were higher than your forecast, that is usually thought of as good news. And it probably is, as long as you're still at the

controls. But don't just accept positive results at face value. Ask, Is the rate of growth acceptable, or are we moving too quickly? Are we moving in the right direction? How does this outcome affect the objective?

2. *Track financial trends essential to the survival of the operation, not just to set new records.* Don't lose sight of the purpose of the financial review. You want to monitor trends and look for problems before they get out of hand. You don't have to surpass results from the previous quarter or year. But you do need to ensure that expansion is built on a solid foundation of your own design, and under your direct control.

3. *Be willing to modify your goals.* Since financial results are best used to judge success—as measured by your own plan— they can also be used to judge how realistically you have planned. If financial results lead you to conclude that your plan is overly optimistic, don't stick to the plan. Modify it. The plan is only a general guide, and once you discover that it isn't working, you need to change it.

* * *

Closely related to the need for coordinating financial results and business objective is the concern most businesses have with customer service. Measuring the customer's response to changes in your operation is an excellent nonfinancial method for identifying the best possible rate of expansion. That's the topic of Chapter 9.

Chapter 9

The Customer Service Approach

You may determine your business objective, define the pace of growth, and set your business on a clear and positive expansion path. But how do you know whether your business is growing in the right direction? The attitude of your customers, who may be the forgotten element in your expansion plan, provides a valuable test of how well you manage growth and how permanent your expansion plan will be.

You need to define *customer service* for yourself, based on the type of business you're running and on how you value the people paying money into that business. A purely financial analysis deals only with numbers. Behind those numbers are real people, with perceptions about who you are and what you offer for sale.

This definition should identify specifically *how* you and your staff serve the customer. It's not enough merely to state that you "offer excellent service" or "quality."

Example: A marketing consultant has expanded her operation over the last two years and now has three additional employees who also provide consultation to clients. Keenly aware of the importance of customer service, she has defined this idea with several rules:

We will save the client more than our services cost.

We will not exceed a project price.

We will always speak directly with the client upon completion of a project, to make sure that client is completely satisfied with the results. If not, we will take all necessary and reasonable steps to achieve complete satisfaction.

We will never miss a promised delivery date.

Example: A retail appliance store offered repair services in addition to sales. The owner ensured customer loyalty with the standard that every repair must be tested before equipment is given back to the customer, that a machine will always be ready by the promised date, and that repair estimates are not exceeded unless additional problems are discovered (in which case, the customer must first be called). He followed up by calling many customers after work was completed, and made sure that they were satisfied with the work his employees had done.

By testing the customer's attitude and satisfaction level, you can decide very quickly if you've been able to hold on to your original objective or if you're moving away from the standard you set for your business. If you ever find yourself unsure of how your operation is perceived by your customers, you are not applying this critical test. Then it's time for you to get back in touch with the customer and find out what he or she thinks. Your advisors, employees, vendors, and competitors all can wait. The customer should go to the top of your priority list—and remain there.

The Customer Service Philosophy

Customer service is just as important a function in your business as are accounting, filing, and secretarial services. When faced with excessive overhead and the need to cut expenses, some companies make the mistake of eliminating the customer service department. But doing away with a customer service function leads only to further erosion of the expanded operation. Or, your day might be consumed with demands from your internal staff, but even in the middle of solving problems,

you can't forget that the customer is at the core of everything
you do.

As the owner of a successful, expanding company, you
will want to define the most important attitudes and ideas
concerning customer service. These include:

1. *Customer service, whether provided by one person or a department, is a high priority.* You can't afford to eliminate or delay
service, because customers are constantly aware of how they're
being treated.

Example: A restaurant owner promoted her business by promising excellent food. But when profit margins began to close, she laid
off several waiters and expected a smaller staff to take care of more
tables. That meant customers were not served as promptly as before,
and business fell off. In that business, the quality of food was not as
important to the customer as was the quality of service.

Example: The owner of a home-improvement store hired several
employees to work a service desk. When customers had questions,
they took a number and received personal attention from one of the
representatives. When a big sale was advertised, the owner doubled
the service crew so that higher traffic would not mean a longer wait
at the service desk.

2. *Service is more important than price.* Your customers will
remember good service and, equally important, will also remember poor service. Differences in price are *not* as important
to the customer as is being treated professionally and
promptly.

Example: The owner of a clothing store could not figure out why
her lower prices did not bring in more business. A competitor down
the street charged about 10 percent more for the same items, but her
volume appeared to be much better. The answer was that the other
owner made sure customers were cared for promptly, and did not
have to wait for service.

Example: A graphic designer promoted his services by offering
to work for $35 per hour, when most of his competitors were charging

$50 and more. Still, he was unable to land several big accounts he targeted. Finally, he realized that the discount pricing did not matter as much as the client's satisfaction with the level of service.

3. *It's sometimes a good investment to lose money instead of a customer.* Don't let your budget rule the way you operate to the exclusion of the bigger picture. Your reputation is much more important than not exceeding a particular month's targeted expense level.

Example: A contractor had bid a job at $16,000, with an allowance for 5 percent net profit, or $800. He was pleased when that goal was met. But when the job was completed, the customer called with a problem. It would take one worker two full days to fix, and that would cut the profit considerably. He realized, though, that the goal was not as important as ensuring that the customer was completely happy with the job.

Example: A retail store owner received a call from a customer, complaining that a delivery had not been made as promised by the manager. The owner called the manager and instructed him to deliver the goods in person and at once; that meant a four-hour round-trip. To the owner, keeping a promise was more important than the cost of having the manager away from the floor for the entire morning, even though the payroll cost exceeded the profit made on the sale.

Accepting a loss today might get you more advertising mileage than an expensive ad campaign. The public remembers stories of corporate customer service, and responds more to those examples than to even the best-designed ads and promises.

Key Questions

When you started your business, you probably paid a lot of attention to the customer, asking yourself who that customer should be, what he or she wanted and was willing to pay for it, and how to best serve that person. The danger is that, with growth, you will forget these all-important questions. Test your awareness by asking the questions again, based on each of the expansion traps described in Part II, as well as the "numbers" trap discussed in Chapter 8.

The Volume Test

Permanent, profitable volume is built when customers (or clients) are satisfied with the service they receive—even after the sale. You will achieve permanent growth when the same people come back to you again. Ask these questions as your business grows:

1. Are my customers loyal, and does my business have the reputation as an excellent service provider?
2. Am I providing the product or service that I intended to provide when I started my business?
3. Do my customers stay with me, or has expansion been accompanied by a higher turnover in customers?
4. What steps have I taken to ensure continuing and improving support to my customers as business has expanded?
5. What additional steps must I take before future expansion occurs?
6. Am I happy with the rate of growth, and am I prepared to offer the same level of customer service even with larger future volume?

The People Test

You manage growth without loss of quality when your employees share your philosophy and treat the customers well. One noteworthy danger signal is a staff that views customer inquiries as an interruption of their day. You need to ensure that your employees put your philosophy of customer service to work every day. One critical element in achieving this is to make sure that your employees are satisfied. Motivated, contented employees are ready to treat customers well; discontented employees are not. Ask these questions:

1. Do my employees care about my customers?
2. Have I defined my personnel policies in writing, and in accordance with current local, state, and federal law?
3. Are my employees content with their working conditions?
4. Is the rate of personnel turnover acceptable to me?
5. What changes must I make to attract and keep the caliber of employees I want?
6. As my internal staff grows, what steps will be necessary to maintain my personal standards for meeting employee needs? How will those needs change as the staff grows?
7. Is there more paper work in the company now than there was a year ago? What steps can I take to reduce the paper flow?
8. Do *all* of my employees understand that they have customers? Do they practice that idea? If not, how can I change the way they work together?
9. Am I able to make decisions based on how the outcome will affect customers? Or am I distracted by what employees and departments want?

The Geography Test

Territorial expansion can lead to a loss of service standards. If you must spend all your time monitoring branch offices or outlets, you can lose touch with what customers want and need, and how well your staff is responding. To ensure the success of territorial expansion, your attention must be on customer service as the most critical, and the most difficult, standard to maintain. Ask these questions:

1. How long has it been since I spoke directly with a customer?
2. Are the managers of remote locations as aware as I am of the need for excellent service (as I have defined it)?
3. What limitations on the rate of growth must I enforce to ensure that customer-service standards are practical?
4. How can I prepare now for maintenance of the cus-

tomer-service standard when territories are even larger in the future?

The Competition Test

If you emphasize customer service, your customer base will grow over time. But if you do not, then your competitors will inherit your customers by out-providing you and permanent growth will not be possible. With expansion, you will no longer be the small company filling the service gap left by larger competitors. You eventually will become one of the larger companies in your industry and other, smaller companies will then pose a threat to you. Whether contending with larger or smaller competitors, ask yourself:

1. Do I provide more than the competition is able or willing to offer?
2. Am I applying the standard that service competition is more important than price competition?
3. How can I ensure that my customers will not go to the competition, even as I expand?
4. What changes should I make now to improve and maintain the same level of service I offered when my company first started out?
5. What does the competition provide to its customers that I do not?

The Financial Test

An analysis of your financial statements, plus the other critical financial tests explained in Chapter 8, will show, to a degree, whether your customers are satisfied. As volume grows, so should profits. Ask yourself:

1. Am I earning *more* profit with growth (created when growth is generated from a base of loyal customers), or am I just expanding the volume of new customers?
2. Am I willing to live with extra expense to keep custom-

ers happy? Or do I allow the profit motive to rule my decisions at the customer's expense?

3. How much time do I spend reviewing financial results, compared to the time I spend with customers (or monitoring the quality of customer service)? How can I increase the time devoted to customers?

4. Do I budget for service-related expenses, or have I tried to cut back to increase net margins?

5. What actions should I take now to improve customer service on all levels, for future expansion plans?

The Declining Quality Trap

As your operation expands into new volume levels, territories, product lines, and outlets, you face the danger that your original concept of service will be lost. What did service mean to you originally, and has your perception changed? More to the point, have you stopped thinking in terms of customer service?

You don't have to accept the notion that *quality*, however you define the word, must decline as your business expands. On the contrary, growth can only be worthwhile when customer service is at the top of your list and if that idea is incorporated into your objective. Most of all, quality and responsiveness have to be a daily practice and an accepted way of going about business, not just an idea.

Is it naïve to think that you can stay in touch with your customers, even when your business has grown beyond a single outlet? In practice, many owners of expanding companies have drifted away from customer contact for several reasons, which might be expressed as:

I've delegated the task of customer contact, because I don't have the time. I'm doing more important things now.
There are too many customers to track.
Customer service is not necessary now that we're a big company.
Customers don't care about service, as long as they can get a lower price than what the competition is offering.

All of these perceptions are false. The trap here is in believing that customer service is only worth the effort while a company is young and that an established operation no longer needs to impress the market. Or that factors like time, volume, and price supersede the need to always place the customer first. But those companies that do expand successfully have one thing in common:

> Management is constantly aware of the absolute priority of keeping the customer happy. You can never be too big, too busy, or too overwhelmed to pay attention to those people or companies that write checks to you.

Example: The owner of a bookkeeping service originally contacted new accounts by writing individual letters to companies, and then following up with direct contact. She started her business before she had a word processor and, over the course of three months, she typed more than 500 letters. Today, she has twelve employees and more than fifty clients. But she still writes her own letters, stays in touch with every customer, and returns every phone call from customers—all in person.

You can delegate many of the time-consuming tasks of maintaining a healthy customer-service attitude. These include applying standards for response time, ensuring accuracy of work, and delivering promised results on time. But as the owner you can also keep in touch, if not with every customer every month, at least through random testing and limited direct contact.

It is not naïve to begin a business with high ideals concerning customer service. Later you might look back to the days when direct contact with every customer was possible, and when volume was low enough that you were able to see customers on a regular basis—and to respond exceptionally well. If you want to achieve lasting growth, that same approach is not only possible, it's essential.

With the pressures of running a business, coordinating cash flow, anticipating problems, and confronting an array of daily problems associated with growth, you can easily lose sight of how important your customer is, and should remain. You might have to remind yourself many times that taking care of the customer is a task that belongs at the top of your list, right next to the function of planning.

As you delegate more day-to-day routines to others, your management task becomes more complicated—if only because you have more to do and less time in which to get it done. But by remembering your objective and your plan, you will discover that customer service is, in fact, tied in with the management roles you play in supervising employees, setting and monitoring the course of expansion, and applying the standards of your business objective.

Tied in with the oversight and planning routines is the very idea of customer awareness. When employees approach you with a new idea, a proposed change in procedures, or a request that requires spending more money, ask yourself two questions:

1. How does this fit with the plan?
2. How does this serve the customer?

Even the most difficult decisions become clear choices when you ask these questions. They address the concerns you have expressed in your objective, assuming that the objective includes the customer.

Service Within the Company

Customer service is usually discussed just in terms of the external customer. But the same philosophy can be applied to each employee in your company. Whenever you hear someone saying, "I'm not in contact with the customer, so customer service is not my job," you should correct the misperception.

Telling employees that they're all working for the customer doesn't do the job. You need to prove to all your employees that they are *directly* involved in customer service in every aspect of their job. Employees who do not have direct contact with customers are not going to believe a slogan or go along with a philosophy just because that's what you'd like. They need proof.

For example, during a manager's meeting, suppose you raise the subject of response time to answer questions from customers. Your bookkeeper comments that he is not involved with the customer. The bookkeeper doesn't ever see a customer—at least not an *external* customer. But you can clarify your message by expanding the definition of *customer*. In reality, the bookkeeper *is* in the customer-service business; his customer is every other department in the company. These departments depend on him to keep the bank account in good order, to comply with federal and state rules, and to prepare and distribute payroll checks.

You can make the same argument for every other employee. Each either serves the public directly or supports that effort by providing a service to another department. A retail stocking clerk who works only after closing time might never have direct customer contact, but his work reflects you and your company, and makes a difference in how customers perceive the organization. The mail-room employee, the secretary, and the maintenance supervisor all have customers within the organization. The standards for service and diligence apply to them as much as a salesperson must satisfy the public customer.

Even if expansion leads to the creation of many departments and reporting layers, you can still make certain that every executive and manager understands the idea of customer service. You might have to repeat the idea many times, and take steps to demonstrate and prove your point, as well as enforce the standard. But the size of your company should not dictate the importance of customer service, nor the need for it.

This customer-service approach can solve many of the internal conflicts and decisions that arise with expansion. Whenever a conflict arises, ask these questions:

1. Who is the customer?
2. What types of service are supposed to be provided, by whom, and for what purpose?
3. Where is the system not working?

4. What steps do I need to take to make sure the customer is being satisfied?

For example, suppose a conflict arises between your sales manager and the office manager. The sales manager complains that checks for commissions and expense reimbursements are delayed and that the office manager doesn't realize the high priorities of paying salespeople. The office manager explains that expense reports are submitted without receipts, or are added incorrectly, and that commissions are paid on a schedule, and exceptions are not allowed. Apply the previous four questions to resolve the problem.

1. *Who is the customer?* The salespeople are the customers of the administrative department. The individual points of view are not the issue, although this argument often deteriorates into one of who is right and who is wrong. While the sales manager should certainly respect office procedures, the office manager will do well to adopt the attitude that the sales department *is* the customer.

2. *What types of service are supposed to be provided, by whom, and for what purpose?* Procedures have been established for handling transactions. Expense reports are supposed to contain verifying receipts, and commissions are paid at predetermined times (weekly, every two weeks). But some compromise might be reasonable. For example, the office manager might be willing to correct math errors on expense reports as part of the customer-service function. And commissions could be paid earlier than scheduled when the amount due exceeds a specified level. These compromises will solve most of the problems that come up.

3. *Where is the system not working?* Because each department has its own point of view, communication is poor. Even though the mechanical system works, the human system does not. But a slight adjustment in attitude will clear up this problem if both sides are willing. For example, the sales manager needs to understand that office management is just as important a function as selling. And the office manager can be

flexible in applying the rules for its customers (like the sales department).

4. *What steps do I need to take to make sure the customer is being satisfied?* In this case, the customer—the sales department—understands only that its operation is being inhibited by procedures. The manager of that department will appreciate the problems faced in the office by going over those procedures with the office manager. The office manager has taken a hard line by not accommodating exceptions.

You can help each department solve the problem by getting them to work together. Problems with procedures can be solved once each manager understands the problems faced by the other. This doesn't mean your task is easy, or that you can solve any problem just by making two people sit down and talk. But once the customer-service approach is appreciated by each side, arriving at a solution is much easier.

Just as you can't respond to every request made by a customer, there are limits in your internal system, too. You can't sell goods below cost just because a customer wants something for less money; so, too, one department has to understand that another has limitations and constraints in the service it can provide. Both sides need to work together, and to respect the rules by which the other must live.

Example: A salesman wanted a commission check right away, but everyone in the accounting department was busy trying to meet a tax return deadline. It's not reasonable to expect a high level of customer service, because other work takes priority.

Example: A salesman submitted an expense report and needed the money as soon as possible. It would take the accounting department only ten minutes to verify math and issue a check. Assigning one person the task of taking care of this would be a small inconvenience to promote good relationships between the two departments.

Building on Your Reputation

When you provide customer service at a higher level than that of your competitors, permanent and successful expansion will be possible. The standard you set on all levels (see Figure 9-1) for the external customer, between internal departments, and between you and your employees can be defined according to the following criteria:

1. *Loyalty* is a large part of establishing your customer-service standard. If you want customer loyalty, you will have to provide loyalty to the customer.

2. *Reputation* is of critical importance to your company, evidenced in the quality of employee service and for you individually. All of these groups have a reputation that can be maintained or are endangered if ignored with future expansion.

3. *Following through on promises* is a very revealing test of whether your customer-service program is real or just so many words. For example, when a customer calls you with a complaint, it's relatively easy to promise satisfaction. Just be sure you come through, promptly and as promised; otherwise, you will do more damage by not honoring your promise.

4. *Monitoring* the assignments you give to others can make or break a customer-service program. You can't be everywhere at once and, in an expanded business, you can't meet every customer. Thus a large part of the day-to-day customer service actions are entrusted to your employees. But by spending enough of your time to monitor the program, you can ensure that your standards are enforced.

Figure 9-1.   Customer-service standards.

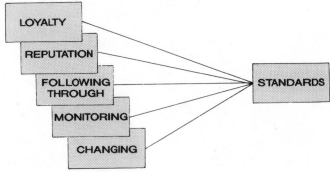

5. *Changing* as your business grows allows you to tailor your service program. When you first started out, it was possible to respond individually to every customer question or complaint. As you expand, you will want to change both the approach and the monitoring system in use, so that you can balance time restraints with the desire to continue putting excellence into action.

*   *   *

While you're busy making sure that your customers and employees are satisfied, you will also want to stay on course with the personal objective you've set for yourself as owner of the business. Your purpose in establishing your independence was to gain personal and financial freedom. Chapter 10 deals with the importance of keeping that freedom while you expand, and of not letting expansion keep you from meeting your personal goals.

Chapter 10

The Expansion Kit

Two people with similar backgrounds, education, experience, and ability opened their own small businesses five years ago. Both operations are profitable. But when you compare the owners' attitudes, you find important differences. One is enthusiastic, motivated, and content; the other is burned out, under constant pressure, and dissatisfied.

Why the differences? What did the first one do right, and where did the second one go wrong? Even though both businesses are succeeding in financial terms, the owners see things very differently. The answer is, one owner has a clear vision of where the business is going and the other does not.

Your morale will depend largely on the degree of control you have over every aspect of your business. If you end up as a passenger rather than as the driver, you can't determine the course and your business takes on a character and objective of its own. As your business expands, you need to develop methods for testing how well you're staying in control and reaching your goals. The expansion kit—a series of tests you apply to yourself—will help you maintain your perspective and modify your schedule and time commitment from day to day.

It's not enough to set goals and reach them. You need to reconcile your financial and personal goals as your operation expands. A dependable test of how well you're doing this is to evaluate your use of time. Are you putting time and energy into the activities you want to pursue? Or is your day taken up with problems that distract you from what you really want?

The Planning Approach

To stay in control, you must make planning your most important activity. Setting and executing goals is not a one-time function or something you can do only at the beginning of the year. Planning should take place every day. Many busy owners resist the idea that they can take one full day a week—or more—to plan. But if you want to create an ideal business environment, planning should become the most important role you play.

Remember these points about planning:

1. *Goals should be reviewed and revised from time to time.* Setting and reaching goals demands constant maintenance. Even the best-defined, most appropriate goal might not work a few months from now. Everything changes, even the direction you want your business to go. But the motive behind your direction will probably remain the same. Your problem is how to adjust to change without losing sight of what you want to achieve.

2. *It's not enough to state your goals once. Your managers and employees—and you—need to be reminded.* One common planning error is to put a lot of energy into defining your direction, and then not following up. One of your best investments in time is to meet with your staff to review your goals and agree (even with yourself) on the direction in which you're moving. Remember, even when you're driving a vehicle in a straight line, you have to keep your hands on the steering wheel or you'll veer off course.

3. *You can retain the sense of freedom that led you into your own business, even when your business environment changes drastically.* One of the nagging problems of growth is that the owner tends to lose control over how time is spent. You face a wider array of problems to solve, your energy and attention are pulled and

pushed in many directions, and the day is characterized by unending pressure. Instead of leading your operation in *your* desired direction, you end up responding to its collective demands.

If this occurs as you expand, it's time to make a few changes. Expansion itself is not the problem, and you don't have to stop growing just to take control over your operation. Instead, take a different approach. Judge the success of an expansion plan by the way you use your day. Are you solving immediate problems when, in fact, you would rather be planning the future?

The Time Test

Each of the three points about planning is tied to the idea that proper use of time is the key to successful expansion. You will want to dedicate your time to:

1. Reviewing and reinforcing personal goals and business direction
2. Reminding yourself where you want your operation to go, and identifying the best way to get there
3. Planning the next expansion phase, rather than responding to daily problems

In addition, you need a mechanism to measure your own success—beyond the study of profit or loss. Financial results are part of the measurement, of course, but your larger concern is with questions of overall direction and control. Are you spending your time the way you want? Are you in control of your day, or is the day controlling you? Do you have the time to look far ahead? Or are you so deeply involved in solving immediate problems that you can't even think about tomorrow?

How much time do you allow yourself for planning? This is one of the most critical functions you can perform, not only to ensure the financial success of your growing business but also to keep it on track with your personal goals. And yet, most small-business owners spend very little time in planning functions. A survey[1] of those in business between three and four and a half years revealed that time was spent in these activities:

Dealing with employees	10%
Direct selling	25%
Production	20%
Financial and record-keeping	20%
Planning	5%
Other activities	20%

When you've been in business for five years or less, the demands of just surviving might make this schedule unavoidable. That's to be expected. But as you expand beyond the initial phases, the division of time needs to change.

It might seem that as volume and territories grow, it will also be necessary for you to spend ever-increasing time in direct selling, production, and record-keeping routines. But if you allow yourself to follow this course, the entire expansion plan will be in jeopardy. Remember:

> As your business expands, planning becomes increasingly important. The other routines can and should be delegated.

If you increase your time commitment to selling and accounting routines, you limit the amount of expansion you can manage. Your time is finite. Your efforts can take you only so far. The time will come when you need to step back from involvement with the day-to-day operations and spend more time plotting your expansion.

You will not want to lose touch with your customers or employees during this shift in commitment. That's a common problem with expansion. You could spend so much time in meetings, on the road, or reviewing internally generated reports that the tone of your business goes off in its own direction and you become a stranger, an outsider, a remote player in your own company.

An alternative is to devote more energy to the planning

phase but to structure that phase so that you do keep in touch. You may include these activities under the heading of planning:

- Direct contact with customers, not to sell but to check on perceptions of quality and service, both during and after the sale.
- Meetings with employees, whose involvement in planning should be active and direct.

Establish a schedule for yourself that puts planning at the top of the list. Giving only 5 percent of your week to planning functions might not be enough. As you expand, you may want to increase that to 20 or 30 percent. One possible division of your time and energy for the fifth through tenth years in business calls for dividing your time in the following way:

Planning	20%
Dealing with employees	20%
Direct selling	15%
Production	10%
Financial and record-keeping	15%
Other activities	20%

Yet another possible schedule is:

Planning	30%
Dealing with employees	25%
Direct selling	10%
Production	10%
Financial and record-keeping	15%
Other activities	10%

Notice that as planning time is increased, so is the time alloted to dealing with employees. The other routines will have to be delegated, meaning you will want to spend more time monitoring what others are doing. Direct selling, production, and financial or record-keeping tasks end up on someone else's desk, but cannot be completely ignored. Expansion demands delegation, and delegation demands supervision. It's a mistake to increase your planning time but ignore the need for reviewing the results of delegation.

Designing Your Own Expansion Kit

The test of success is a matter of personal standards. Your plan will combine financial and personal measurements, judged not once per year but constantly. Chapter 8 introduced a number of financial testing devices beyond the traditional financial statements:

1. Sales forecasts
2. Cost and expense budgets
3. Cash-flow projections
4. Cash-flow analysis
5. Key account analysis
6. Ratio and trend tests

When you review these numbers and then combine those results with nonfinancial attributes, you have a means for planning. Your expansion kit (see Figure 10-1) should include an examination of qualities discussed in the following sections.

Vision

If you study other companies that have expanded successfully, you will notice they all have one thing in common: a specific, well-expressed philosophy. The owner stated the views that became the foundation for the company's objective. Vision is the premise for growth. It keeps the company on track, it narrows the focus and directs the energy, keeps distractions at bay, and exposes expansion pitfalls.

You started your business with a vision, probably a very strong one. As your business expands, this vision should not be lost in the ever-increasing level of activity. It should be strengthened and made the central theme of expansion. It can define and clarify what you expect from employees and keep you on the right course.

Figure 10-1. Worksheet: problem-solving questions.

1. VISION

What solution will conform to the vision I have for my company?

_____

_____

_____

2. PATIENCE

Must the solution be immediate? What are the alternatives?

_____

_____

_____

3. PERSPECTIVE

Does this problem alter my perspective?

_____

_____

_____

4. ENTHUSIASM

What solution can be developed with enthusiasm?

_____

_____

_____

5. FLEXIBILITY

Do the old methods work, or is it time to change?

_____

_____

_____

To plan with focus, ask yourself this key question whenever you confront a difficult problem:

> What solution will conform to the vision I have for my
> company?

Patience

Expansion takes time. Many people have tried to create big
businesses overnight, only to run into serious problems. You
can enjoy the expansion process for the rewards it brings, but
only if you're willing to support your growth with the people,
systems, and gradually increasing market loyalties you will
need.

Opportunities for rapid, profitable, and successful expansion do present themselves, but this is the exception rather
than the rule. A handful of companies have been able to grow
rapidly *and* successfully, usually because an original idea came
along at just the right time. But it's much more likely that you
will need to patiently nurture your business as it grows.

In arriving at solutions, remember that not every problem
has to be solved right away. In some cases it's better to back
away and wait for the right time. Ask yourself:

> Must the solution be immediate, or can I afford to wait for
> a better opportunity to address this issue?

Perspective

As your business expands, so will your point of view. Some of
your original beliefs may have changed, or you may now see
things in a completely new way. Your perspective will change;
you will grow with your business.

This positive experience can also become a pitfall. Because
you change as your operation expands, you need to ask yourself a series of questions, if only to ensure that you're still
following a positive growth path. These include:

> *What do I want to achieve?*
> *Is my objective still valid?*
> *Is the objective working?*

How have my personal goals changed?
What actions must I take today?
How can I improve my use of time?
What's going wrong, and how can I fix it?
What's going right, and how can I repeat it?

If your perspective is clear, solutions come easily. But if you find yourself reacting to the immediate problem, your solutions might not conform to your expansion plan. When trying to solve problems, ask yourself:

> Does this problem alter my perspective on how my business should operate, or might it lead to a new and improved perspective?

Enthusiasm

Nothing is as inspiring as working for an enthusiastic leader. When you convey your energy to those who work for you, many of the problems associated with growth will disappear on their own. For example, enthusiasm will keep you energetic, allow you to follow up on delegation while inspiring and motivating others, and keep you constantly aware of personal goals. Enthusiasm and focus are attributes of strong leaders, and they are powerful tools for taking a small company along the expansion path.

When you're enthusiastic, no problem is too large or too difficult. When confronting the difficult issues, always ask yourself:

> How can I solve this problem with enthusiasm for the solution, rather than settle for a compromise that distracts from my goals?

Flexibility

Not only will the internal environment evolve as you expand, but the very way you conduct business will change as well.

With future advances in technology, evolving employee attitudes and motivations, and changes in the economic climate,
you will want to keep in touch and review critical issues with a
fresh point of view. This requires personal flexibility. You may
come to the time when you'll question not only the direction
of business but your personal goals as well. And you may want
to change.

You may need to break away from traditional thinking in
the future. One of the problems of running your own business
is that you can lose touch with the way other companies are
run, with emerging attitudes, and with methods of competing.
The Kiplinger Washington editors predict:

> The challenge to business management over the
> next two decades will be coping with change more
> rapid and deep than ever encountered before.
>
> The forces of change sweeping through the
> economy won't allow much time for contemplation
> or foot-dragging.
>
> The swiftness of change will put an extra pre-
> mium on agility and quickness of response. Com-
> panies both enormous and tiny will retune their
> command structures to fit new ways of doing busi-
> ness and of stimulating innovation, while keeping
> step with the needs and demands of new genera-
> tions of employees.[2]

Solve the most difficult business decisions by questioning
your own approach. Be willing to change if new information
dictates. Develop solutions by asking:

> Can the problem be resolved using the same methods
> applied in the past, or is it time to change my methods?

*   *   *

Asking yourself the right questions opens the door to a creative
approach. By applying these attributes to solve problems, you
can widen the possible alternatives. When you started your

business, you discovered the chance to try out new ideas; as you grow, these ideas can be put into practice.

The Success Test

Traditional methods for monitoring success are useful but incomplete. Being on track with your forecast and budget, earning what you consider an acceptable profit, and maintaining a balance between expansion goals and cash flow are vital to survival. But they address only part of what success should include. You complete the success evaluation by combining the financial tests with the nonfinancial factors that matter as well. For example, your effectiveness as a problem solver ultimately determines whether you will be able to make your business expand. In defining success for yourself, what are the elements that fulfill your expectations?

Widen the scope of your expansion kit by developing your own success test. Set standards for what you consider acceptable financial results and acceptable use of your time. Use a worksheet to capture what you consider the most important financial and nonfinancial tests of success. Such a worksheet is shown in Table 10-1. However, the table is just a sample, and does not necessarily express the goals *you* need to evaluate yourself. Complete your worksheet at the beginning of the year and review it at least each month. (More frequent review may be appropriate when expansion is bringing rapid change to your operation.) Use the results of this exercise to guide your future actions.

As a second phase, compare the results each month to your proposed success goals, and decide whether those results are acceptable or unacceptable. Use a worksheet to summarize what you consider the key tests of your financial goals.

The worksheet shown in Table 10-2 does not replace the detailed financial analysis you need to perform each month. Instead it summarizes results so that you can perform a review and answer the question, Am I on the right course? The answer is rarely yes or no. You will discover specific areas demanding attention and action. Success is achieved as the combination of

---

Table 10-1.   Worksheet for successful expansion.

---

1. This year's sales volume will be between $ _____ and $ _____.

2. I will allow staff increases this year between _____ and _____ people.

3. Fixed overhead this year will be between $ _____ and $ _____.

4. My time this year will be spent in the following activities:

	minimum %	maximum %
Planning	_____	_____
Dealing with employees	_____	_____
Direct selling	_____	_____
Production	_____	_____
Financial/record-keeping	_____	_____
Other activities	_____	_____

5. Things I want to change this year:

a. _____

b. _____

c. _____

d. _____

e. _____

---

many small steps. The worksheet tells you how well your goal is being met monthly, and helps you monitor your success as you proceed from one month to the next.

Your focus will be clear when you apply the success test regularly. If you're so busy solving day-to-day problems that you don't have time to look at the bigger picture, then you can't plan effectively and you won't be able to correct emerging negative trends. Spending time each week in testing degrees of success will remind you of your goal and help you stay focused on what you want.

The success test is also a form of self-review. Employees expect evaluations, and want successful job performance rewards via salary increases and promotions. But who does your evaluation? The success test solves that problem; it allows you to identify degress of success, to see your goals being reached, and to put planning control within reach.

Expansion is conceived of and brought to maturity when you understand where you're going and what results you want. Growing too rapidly and then being forced to retreat is not real expansion. It's a misdirected attempt, usually accompanied by a loss of focus. Those who have tried and failed might label expansion as a dangerous and unrewarding experience, but in truth they have never really gone through the expansion process.

Taking risks is necessary to achieve expansion, but only when you know and accept those risks can you crate your own success story. Taking calculated risks is essential to the process; being in control at every step is the only way to maintain an expanding operation.

*   *   *

With thoughtful planning, the day arrives for profitable, controlled expansion, and you are ready. You hire new employees and create a middle management layer. You lease a larger office and buy new furniture and equipment. Your product lines and geographic limits spread. The pace quickens and so does the excitement. The risks increase, and just keeping things running becomes more complicated. But that's not a problem, because you know exactly where you're going and

Table 10-2.   Financial review.

Month _____

	Acceptable?	
	Yes	_No_
1. Sales were _____ % above (below) forecast.	_____	_____
2. Costs and expenses, overall, were ___ % above (below) budget.	_____	_____
3. Receivables are ___ % current and ___ % past due.	_____	_____
4. Were asset and liability accounts analyzed? _____ yes _____ no	_____	_____
5. Were key ratios within an acceptable range? _____ yes _____ no	_____	_____

Action steps:

_____

_____

_____

_____

_____

exactly what's going on—how your customers see you, how satisfied your employees are, and the next step you will take. You're in command.

Notes

1. National Federation of Independent Business survey results, cited in the *Wall Street Journal*, May 15, 1989.
2. Kiplinger Washington Editors, *The New American Boom* (Washington, D.C.: Kiplinger, 1986), p. 206.

Index

account analysis, 151–152
action plan, 18–26
advertising literature, 132–133
advice, 11, 20–21
aging list, 150
asset expansion, 41–42
assumptions, budget, 146
attributes of success, 45–47
automation, 10, 19

budgeting
   assumptions, 146
   cost and expense tests, 145–147
   geographic expansion, 115, 122
   rules checklist, 77
bureaucracy, 22

career paths, employee, 99–102
cash flow
   analysis, 149–151
   planning, 122–123
   projections, 147–149
   standards, 29
cash management procedures, 121–122
checklist
   budgeting rules, 77

competing effectively, 128
competitive guidelines, 137
conditions for expansion, 31
geographic expansion controls, 121
knowing the competition, 133
large competitor disadvantages, 127
review standards, 39
signs of staffing problems, 90
staying healthy, 9
steps to helping employees, 101
taking positive action, 37
competition
   and customers, 129, 133, 135–136, 137
   disadvantages, 127
   effective, 128
   expansion factors, 42, 136–138
   focus, 130
   formulas, 134
   identification, 126–130
   knowledge, 132–134
   management, 134
   myths, 130–132
   strength, 129
   test, 166
   timetable, 129–130
conditions for expansion, 31–34

conflicts between departments, 92

consultants, 15, 24–25

controls, 12–13, 22

current ratio, 152

customer
  diversification, 8–10
  expectations, 18, 137
  loyalty, 8, 135–136

customer service
  competition test, 166
  decline, 167–169
  definition, 160–161
  financial test, 166–167
  geographic expansion, 124–125
  geography test, 165–166
  key questions, 163–164
  people test, 164–165
  philosophy, 161–163
  reputation, 172–174
  standards, 173
  volume test, 164
  within the company, 169–172

debt, 10, 19–20

debt/equity ratio, 154

declining quality, 167–169

delegation, 107–108

departmental mentality, 87–89

diversification, 18–19

educational expenses, 102–103

eliminating lines of business, 82–83

employee
  career paths, 99–102
  conflicts, 92
  educational expense, 102–103
  equity, 101
  expansion, 42, 86–87, 93–94
  goals, 100
  growth problems, 89–96
  incentives, 103
  influence, 96–97
  involvement, 14, 24, 105
  job definitions, 101
  meetings, 94–95
  mentality, 87–89
  personal expansion, 102–103
  planning, 87
  power, 96–97
  promotions, 100
  rewards, 101
  self-interest, 91–92
  seminars, 103
  solutions, 97–99
  talent, 14–15, 24
  test, 164–165
  training, 102
  trends, 104–105
  turnover, 95–96

enthusiasm, 183

equity sharing, 101

excellence, 46–47

executive layers, 94

expense and profit relationship, 73

facility expansion, 41

financial
  controls, 120–123
  facts, 157–158
  flaws, 156–157
  review worksheet, 188
  standards, 158–159
  tests, 141–156, 166–167

flexibility, 183–184

forecasting, sales test, 143–145

geographic expansion
  budgeting, 115
  capital, 111–112
  comparisons, 115

control, 120–125
costs, 115
desirability, 106–110
direction, 114–117
and remote outlets, 120–125
research, 114–115
resources, 115
risk, 110–112
speed, 112–114
staffing, 112
test, 165–166
and turnover, 116
goals, employee, 100
gross margin, 69–70
gross profit, 69
growth
paper work, 90–91
plateaus, 5–8
problems, 89–90
rapid, 93
and self-interest, 91–92
valid, 39–42

healthy
growth, 8
volume curve, 70, 72
home-based workers, 104

identifying the competition,
126–130
image, 117–120
incentives, education, 103
income statement tracking worksheet, 74
influence problems, 96–97
insurance, 14, 23–24
inventory turnover ratio, 116–
117, 154

job definitions, 101

lines of business, 82–83

Management by Objective
(MBO), 52–53
management standards, 30
market research, 114–115
meetings, 94–95
methods of expansion, 41–42
middle management, 91–92, 93–
94
misdirected thinking, 38–39
multiple-outlet expansion, 109–
110
myths about competition, 130–
132

nonfinancial
controls, 123–125
tests, 141–143

objective
absence of, 54–55
approaches, 54–58
definition, 44–45, 49–52
elements, 50
examples, 48–49
and excellence, 46–47, 138
focusing, 45–46
retaining, 58–61
right, 56–58
success, 46
wrong, 56–58
overhead expansion, 42

patience, 182
permanent growth, 40–41
personal expansion, employee,
102–103
perspective, 182–183
positive action, 37–39
power problems, 96–97
product
expansion, 41
lines of business, 82–83
objectives, 50

profit
  margin, 70, 71
  standards, 29
profitable
  debt, 10
  expansion, 30–31
  volume, 40
promotions, 100

quality
  declining, 167–169
  and image, 117–120
  standards, 124
quick assets ratio, 152–153

ratio
  current, 152
  debt/equity, 154
  inventory turnover, 154
  quick assets, 152–153
  turnover in working capital,
    153–154
  working capital, 153
regional comparisons, 118
remote outlets, 120–125
resisting growth, 61–63
rewarding employees, 101
risk
  business, 30
  geographic, 110–112
  selection, 13–14, 23

sales forecast testing, 143–145
scorekeeping
  account analysis, 151–152
  assumptions, 146
  budgets, 145–147
  cash-flow analysis, 149–151
  cash-flow projections, 147–149
  facts, 157–158
  flaws, 156–157
  forecasts, 143–145

ratios, 152–156
standards, 158–159
tests, 141–143
trends, 152–156
seminars, employee, 103
service
  expansion, 41
  lines of business, 82–83
  objectives, 50
simplicity, 13
site evaluation, 117
spending habits, 15, 25
staffing
  problems, 90
  solutions, 97–99
success test, 185, 187

tax planning, 15, 25
time
  commitment, 124
  test, 177–180
tracking record, 76
training programs, 102
trend testing, 152–156
turnover
  employee, 95–96
  inventory, 116–117, 154
  working capital, 153–154

unhealthy volume curve, 71

vision, 180, 182
volume
  comparisons, 72
  curves, 70, 71
  directions, 68–78
  expansion plans, 83–85
  indicators, 68–70
  profitable, 40
  and simplicity, 79–82
  and success, 78–79
  test, 164

working capital ratios, 153
worksheet
   aging list, 150
   assumption, 146
   cash-flow projections, 148
   financial review, 188

income statement tracking, 74
problem-solving questions,
   181
regional comparisons, 118
site evaluation, 117
successful expansion, 186